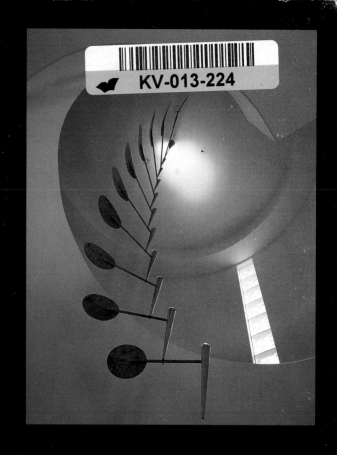

CONTENTS

INTRODUCTION

While attending trade shows and fairs for other purposes, one theme kept standing out — lighting. Again and again I kept drifting into booths where artists were displaying their ingenuity in objects wired for utility, but designed as sculpture.

In an age when homeowners are experiencing unprecedented prosperity in the West, today's designers are free of the idea that lighting is a mere household necessity. They've been given license to create whimsical, playful objects that may just illuminate an owner's individuality more so than the room they call home.

This book doesn't uncover any one trend, but rather highlights artists who are walking their own paths, from those who are crafting minimalist fixtures with space-age precision to those who are bending branches and hand-casting paper and clay. It celebrates artists who take a free hand in creating outrageously colorful objects of play, as well as those still crafting classical pieces fit for Versailles. There are artists here who've drawn inspiration from afar, with pieces inspired by Asian tradition or tropical island atmosphere, as well as the depths of the ocean and the heights of outer space. And while some stretch for the future in their designs, others take us back to more nostalgic times.

Classifying these lamps and lumping them together in chapters was the most difficult task in this book. The objects pictured are each so unique, it was difficult throwing them all into the same pot. Still, it is hoped that the connoisseur enjoying this book will take time to ponder the individual lamps, and forgive the author for trying to place them among diverse peers.

Though many of the objects illuminated in this book are high end, others are surprisingly affordable. All reflect a buyer's willingness to go beyond the ordinary in order to make their home or office unique.

It is hoped that this book will help bring artist together with consumer, whether you are an interior designer, architect, or simply a sophisticated homeowner with heightened good taste. To this end, I have included a resource guide at the back of the book to make contacting these companies and designers as simple as possible. The dimensions of the objects pictured are given to make it easier to fit them into your lives. And suggested retail pricing is given.

I hope that all find this gallery of pictures illuminating and inspiring.

RETRO/NOSTALGIC

Archaic Smile, Inc.
"Spliggle Atomic Shades" in various colors provide retro feel above formed wire bases. Large lamps stand 21" tall, $84.

Archaic Smile, Inc.
"Swizzle Stick" lamp with hand-printed and laced shade on aluminum base stands 21" tall, $84.

Archaic Smile, Inc.
The "Tiki Totem" lamp illuminates a home "Tiki Bar" and "Tiki Mirror." The lamp is 21" tall, $84.

Fantarte
A duck decoupage decorates the shade of this wall sconce. 10" x 9" tall, $36.

Donovan Design
"Signature Deco" and the fringed "Honolulu Deco" lamps stand 24" tall, with solid shade, $490.
With hand-painted geometric print, $1,500.

George Kovacs Lighting, Inc.
"American Continuum" desk lamp designed by Robert Sonneman and crafted of leaded glass. 21" x 27", $500. Pendant, 8" x 6.4" x 4", $1,000.

Kremer Glassworks
A handmade library lamp draws its design inspiration from the Arts and Crafts Movement. 22" x 18" x 18", $800.

George Kovacs Lighting, Inc.
Antique office effect is created with this "Pita Wall" unit, which extends up to 21" and has a 5" backplate, $225.

Casanova/Bjorlin "Tablelights" come in handstitched leather (black, dark chocolate brown, or palomino), in glossy mid-century style laminate (black or white), and in aged mirror. Heights range from 6" x 13", 8" x 19", and 10" x 25" inches, $200-500.

Christopher Poehlmann Studio, Inc.
Made from salvaged mid-century melamine dinner-ware, these lamps are available in varying color combinations, with nickel or brass armature. "Cup and Saucer Chandelier" with gold or silver swag cord and chain and flicker flame bulbs, 14" x 17", suggested retail, $400. "Cup and Saucer Sconce," 6" x 6" x 9", $80.

David Long
TWO AT LEFT: "Kitchen Lamps" with round and cone shades. Once common aluminum kitchen implements get a new life as lighting. 18-24" x 3-6", $225.

LOWER LEFT: "Space Capsule Lamp" draws its distinctive shape from a ricer commonly used in the 1930s and '40s. 16" x 10", $175.

Fantarte
A brass base with whimsical accouterments creates an antique effect for a three-bulb table lamp with cloth shade. 20" tall, $115.

Fantarte
A brass base supports a classically designed, one-sided shade of cloth. 21" tall, $52.

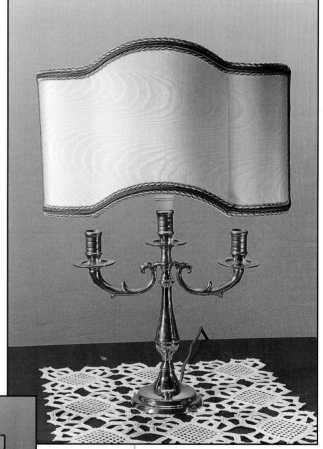

Fantarte
A brass wall lamp supports two bulbs behind a cloth shade. 22" x 36". Sugggested retail: $104.

Fantarte
Modelled on an antique candelabra design, this brass base supports a one-sided shade of cloth. 30" tall, $52.

McLain Wiesand
"Ram's Head Mirrored Sconce" molded from antique mirror with added arms and framing of steel, stamped steel, and resin, shown with antique gilt finish. 20.25" x 14.5" x 3". Available as candle sconce or with electric wiring, $475-625.

Fantarte
Brass base and parchment shade create a classic look for this two-bulb table lamp. 21" tall, $115.

Schonbek World-wide Lighting
In a bathroom as self-indulgent as anything in ancient Rome, the "Colonade" chandelier reflects the architectural theme. 19" x 21" long, $2,250.

Schonbek Worldwide Lighting
"Olde World" chandelier recalls styles popular in nineteenth-century Bohemia. Here it hangs in a French manor style house, with room design by Camille Waldron, ASID. 48" x 62" long, $31,500.

Schonbek Worldwide Lighting
A genteel air of aniquity was achieved with all-new furnishings, including the "Versailles" chandelier, inspired by the French court of Louis XIV. 45" x 52" long, $15,000.

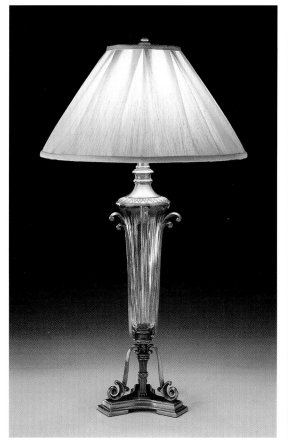

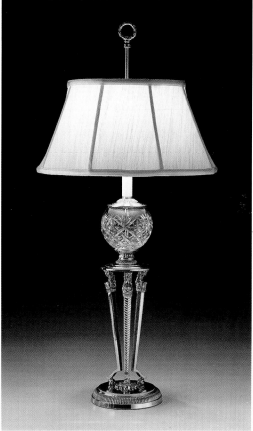

Schonbek Worldwide Lighting/Sierra Custom Builders
Crystal adds elegance to this dining alcove in a chandelier called "Equinoxe." Here the traditional eight-point star shapes found in ancient mosaic patterns create the impression of a massive crystal sculpture of purely contemporary inspiration. 30" x 36" long, $7,500.

Decorative Crafts Inc.
FAR LEFT: Antique brass and crystal lamp with scroll motif and round, off-white fabric shade. 18" x 31.75", $300.

LEFT: Lacquered brass lamp with cut crystal sphere, round off-white fabric shade. 17" x 34.5", $250.

Worlds Away
Hand painted tin, tole
style. 26" tall, $260.

*Decorative
Crafts Inc.*
Openwork
lamp with
antiqued
brass finish
and round
off-white
fabric shade.
20" x 30",
$400.

MacKenzie-Childs, Ltd.
"Argentina Spiral Lamp,"
handmade and decorated
terracotta lamp with beaded
shade. 18" x 32", $725.

MacKenzie-Childs, Ltd.
Majolica "Rabbit Warren Floor
Lamp" with mahogany base.
76" x 24", $3,400.

Dez Ryan Studio
Hand-blown glass bodies support shades of silk. "Chinoise," 29" tall, and "Jungle," 24" tall, $650 each.

Dez Ryan Studio
The "Pirate Polka Meistboy" lamp is a limited edition piece embodying designer Dez Ryan's work, here with a Victorian feeling. 37" tall, $1,700.

FLOS USA Inc.
Plisse cloth on a steel frame softens light to a warm glow on this "Romeo SoftFloor" fixture. An inner egg-shaped glass diffuser has been etched to help with the softening process, and a touch dimmer gives the user full control. 63" tall, $1,295.

Cherry Tree Design
From the Gallery Collection. Crafted for wood lovers, these matching floor lamps, 62" tall, $589.
Table lamps, of solid cherry to provide three-dimensional relief. The wood shade is joined together by lap joints with a fibrous Frost insert. 16" x 25", $499.

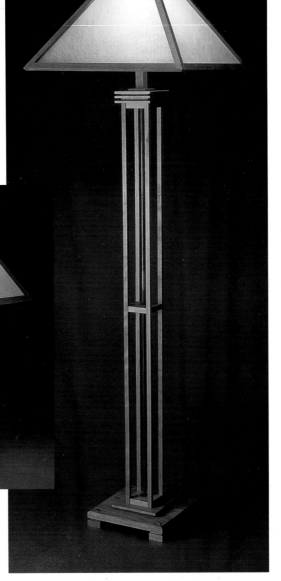

Fantarte
Floor lamp of burnished brass and tiffany glass flowers stands approximately 5' tall, $390.

Cherry Tree Design
The "Arbor" table lamp with wood shade, and fibrous Forest paper insert. Solid cherry construction. 25" tall, $360.

Cherry Tree Design
An Amber Mica insert in this solid wood shade adds depth of color above a solid oak or cherry base. 25" tall, $360.

EXOTIC

Worlds Away
A touch of foliage adds a tropical feel to this long and lean table lamp in three color variations. 20" tall, $140.

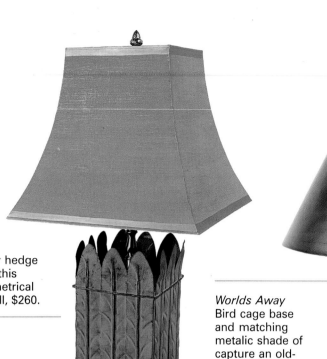

Worlds Away
A tropical privacy hedge forms a base for this captivatingly symetrical table lamp. 25" tall, $260.

Worlds Away
Bird cage base and matching metalic shade of capture an old-world charm. 22" tall, $210.

Cotule
ABOVE: Woven stainless steel and bronze mesh shade on bowed wood frame gives this ceiling fixture an aura of Asian craftsmanship. 48" x 48" x 24", $3,800.

LEFT: Two towering floor lamps create starkly different figures. In the foreground, opaque strips of white linen on a body of bent wire give almost human form to luminous "Lipari" floor lamp. In the background, a graceful shade tops the slender "Panarea" lamp.
Lipari, 52" x 14", $2,500.
Panarea, 60" x 17", $1,350.

Cherry Tree Design
Rice paper and wood combine for an Oriental flavor in this geometric pendant. 8.5 x 14" tall, $219.

Cherry Tree Design
A multi-ringed framework and solid wood top create this complimentary wall sconce. 8.5" x 18", $299; and table lamp, 8" x 12", $239. Available in various woods and finishes.

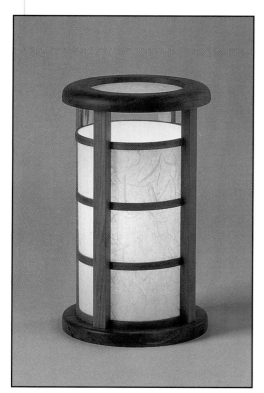

Cherry Tree Design
Pagoda-style pendant of paper and wood. 13" x 20" tall, $369.

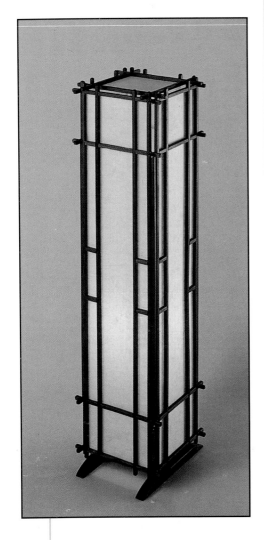

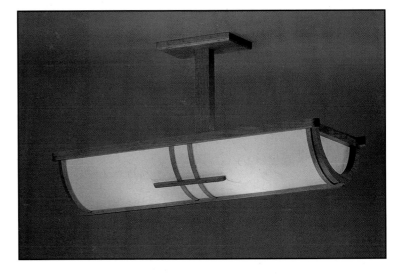

Cherry Tree Design
ABOVE: Wood and paper are held together by tension joints. 11" x 40" tall, $549.

ABOVE RIGHT: three-light chandelier of cherry with Ocean Mist Paper Shade. 36" wide, $988.

RIGHT: Ceiling fixture of hand-crafted wood and paper. 11" x 30" x 16", $450.

Sculture in Luce
TOP LEFT: A copper spiral base supports a lotus of white silk cotton paper. 14" tall, $150.

LEFT: A mangrove root supports a stunning fantasy flower. 28" tall, $330.

BELOW LEFT: Gold and blue tones unite in this paper and copper sculpture, lit from within. 36" tall, $190.

BELOW: A pink lotus blooms from a mangrove root, supported by a copper wire and foil structure. 14" tall, $210.

Sculture in Luce
A mangrove root topped by a fantastic bloom of silk-cotton paper. 22" x 10", $200.

Sculture in Luce
A vegetable extract creates a marbled rose effect on silk-cotton paper, sculpted into a flower on a copper frame and natural tree root. 20" tall, $200.

George Kovacs Lighting, Inc.
Wrought iron effect gives a Spanish feel to the "Inezgane Pendant," available in black, white, or rust with natural parchment diffuser. 29.5" x 11.5", $150. Matching wall sconce, 9", $310.

George Kovacs Lighting, Inc. "Moonage" ceiling fixture uses primitive symbols in bronze rustique or blackened iron setting surrounding white excavation glass shade. 23" x 22", 10' adjustable wire and cable, $625.

George Kovacs Lighting, Inc. Iron Twist chandelier is a dance of russet metal with amber excavation glass shade, designed by Robert Sonneman. 33" x 22", 10' adjustable wire and cable, $685.

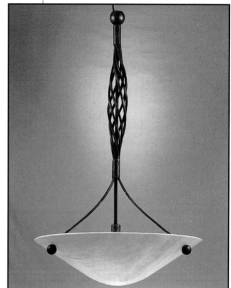

George Kovacs Lighting, Inc. Matching tripod floor lamp and table lamp with a tribal feel, available in antique black chip or silver leaf chip. Floor lamp, 70" x 21", $625. Table lamp, 27" x 10", $810.

George Kovacs Lighting, Inc.
Floor lamp stands on a cloverleaf of swirled metal, also available in antique black or gold leaf with a gold shade. 52" x 15", $560.

George Kovacs Lighting, Inc.
Canyon series lamps designed by Robert Sonneman utilize a shade of natural hay crepe and woven iron bases.
Table lamp: 34" x 22", $485.
Floor lamp: 63" x 22", $500.

George Kovacs Lighting, Inc.
Wall sconce and chandelier to complement
the Canyon series. Sconce, 14" x 19", $985.
Chandelier, 22" x 27", $435.

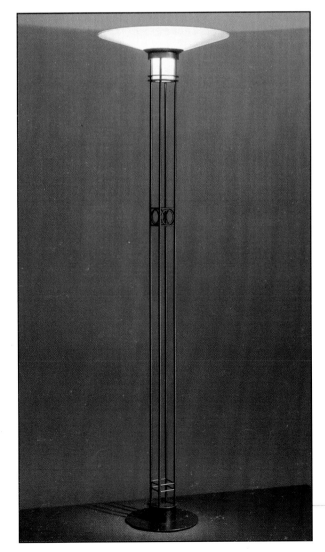

George Kovacs Lighting, Inc.
"Prairie Rings" floor lamp and pendant come
in finishes of weathered gun metal, bronze, or
black. Floor lamp, 71" x 20" glass shade, $685.
Pendant, 21" x 20", $810.

George Kovacs Lighting, Inc.
Named "Maximilian Hunderwasser," this playful design by Dennis Higgins defies straight lines while being very upright. 40" x 13", $310.

George Kovacs Lighting, Inc.
"Urban Primitive" wall sconce and floor lamp make a statement in weathered gun metal, burnished brass, and crushed parchment. Floor lamp, 58" x 11" base, $500. Sconce, 19" x 7" base, $435.

George Kovacs Lighting, Inc.
Mica-tone glass, soft curves, and mixed metals mark this set of lamps.
Torchiere, 73" x 12" base, $1,000.
Table lamp, 23" x 18" glass shade, $685.
Sconce: 8.5" x 17", $485.

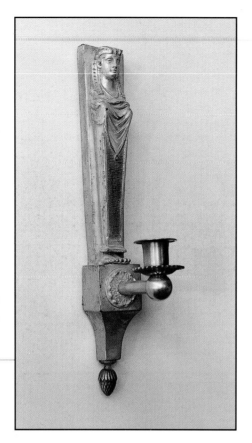

McLain Wiesand
Egyptial wall sconce was molded from a 19th century French mantel clock. Available as a one-, two-, or three-arm electrified sconce. 12.25" x 2" x 4", $750-900/pair.

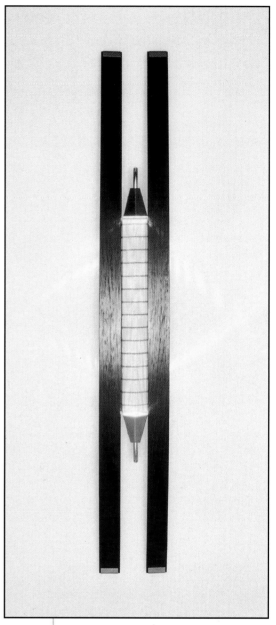

Cotule
Bowed framework houses a glowing woven metal cylinder in this wall sconce from the Millettia Collection. 44" x 6" x 6", $1,750.

Bone Simple Design
Designer Chad Jacobs was playing with the texture of light in these cutouts. Double layers of polypropylene diffuse light from these wall sconces, built on a simple steel wire frame. From the Flexion Series. 12" x 12", $80.

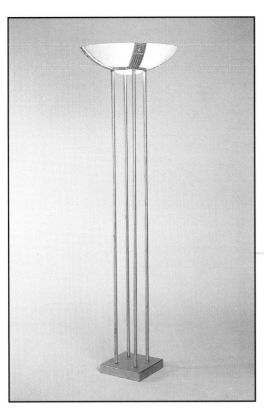

Sirmos
"Coco," a versatile floor lamp from the Vogue Collection, has a hand-painted alabaster resin bowl atop four elegantly thin supports of metal with an antique gold-leaf finish. 72" x 23", $2,682.

Kremer Glassworks
Contemporary interpretations of classic Shoji lanterns were handcrafted by Martin Kremer of American art glass. 14-24", $165

WHIMSICAL

TOP:
David Long
Designed to drive monsters from children's rooms at night, this "Cabin Lamp" is peopled with imaginary Monster Fighters who stay up all night keeping watch. 7" x 8" x 14", $245.

LOWER LEFT:
Sculture in Luce
Dubbed "Libellula," this firefly coils from a green stone on copper tubing. Multi-colored marbles in a half mask diffuse the light. 26" tall, $200.

LOWER RIGHT:
Fantarte
A wall sconce incorporating the design of Oliviero Dallasta creates a colorful, primitive scene. 16" tall, $235.

Fantarte
LEFT: Ribbons suspend this whimsical wall sconce, festooned with a heart-themed decoupage. 25" x 20", $88.

Fantarte
BELOW: A brass table lamp is decorated with tiffany glass or murano beads for colorful effect. 14" tall, $52.

Christopher Poehlmann Studio, Inc. Made from post-consumer clear sheet acrylic, recycled by Christopher Poehlmann Studio into twelve color options, "Crush™" has a steel tripod base and stands a diminutive 18" x 9", $250.

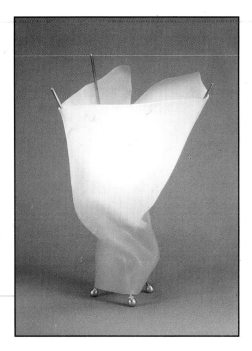

Christopher Poehlmann Studio, Inc. "Mantis™" table lamp has a steel base supporting slightly-off kilter diffusers of hand-colored post-consumer plexiglass. Two sizes: 36" x 12", $290. 19" x 8", $190.

Christopher Poehlmann Studio, Inc. "Popsicle Pendants™" of post-consumer acrylic create a party atmosphere in three sizes: 16" x 3.5", 9" x 4.5", and 16" x 4.5", $150-170.

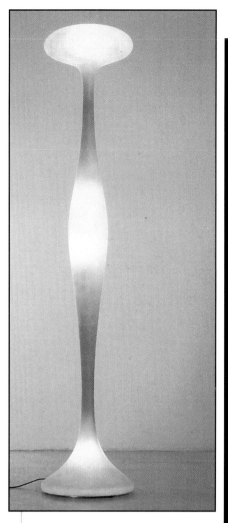

Kundalini "Eta," a sensual column of fiberglass with a metallic inner structure, stands 6.5 feet off the floor. Available in a rainbow of colors, $700-800.

Kundalini
ABOVE: These ceiling fixtures of fiberglass with a polycarbonate reflector and metallic inner structure, are available in eight colors. 21.5" tall, $400.

Kundalini
This funky table lamp design found its way into the second blockbuster Austin Powers movie, but its roots and inspiration go back to Zen with a gesture that transmits the ultimate truth. Made of molded resin; seven colors available. 14" tall, $200.

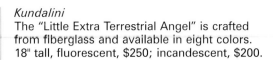
Kundalini
The "Little Extra Terrestrial Angel" is crafted from fiberglass and available in eight colors. 18" tall, fluorescent, $250; incandescent, $200.

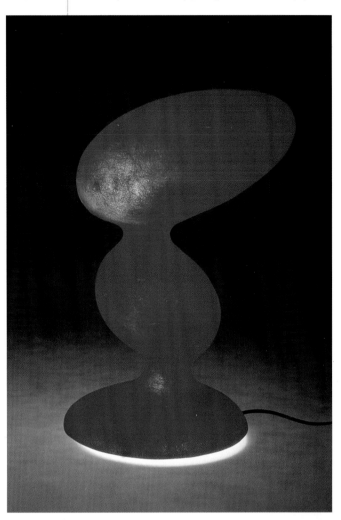

Kundalini
Collapsible lamp with white silk diffuser forms a cone shape when activated. A fan is placed in the molded resin base. 20" tall, $200.

Kundalini
The "Bios" lamp can be used as a table lamp or mounted on the wall. As shown, the fiberglass shade goes from solid to opaque when activated. 16" in diameter, $150

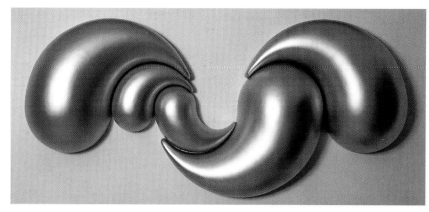

Kundalini
Modular wall brackets of fiberglass allow infinite combinations of luminous arabesques. Available in three sizes (ranging from the largest at 35" x 26" to the smallest at 17.5" x 13") and seven colors, plus a silver version. The silver color is shown both unlit and lit, large, $160; medium, $100; small, $80.

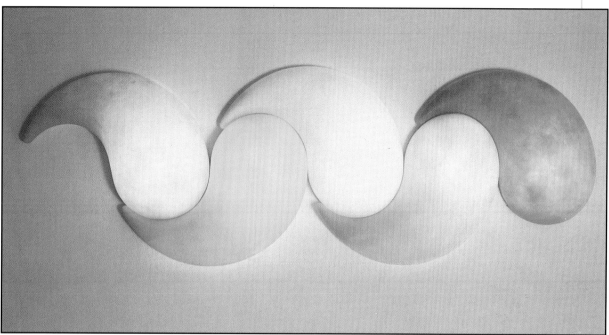

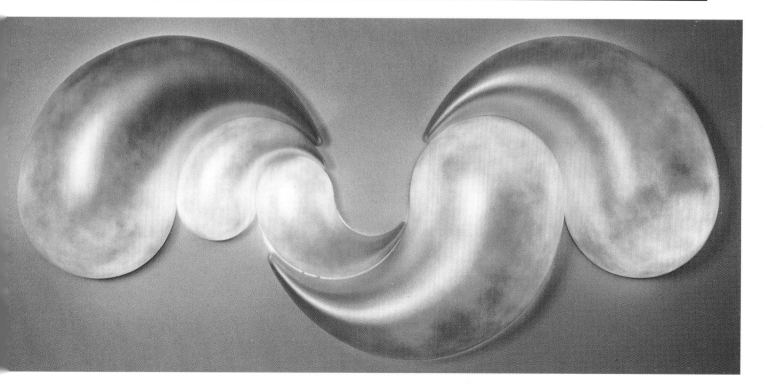

Christopher Poehlmann Studio, Inc. A custom welded salvaged steel base anchors a narrow shade of hand-colored, post-consumer acrylic shade on the "Monolith™." 33" x 8", $570.

Tiny Flame Studio
Ranging in height from 16" to 24", these versatile lamps were designed to either hang from gold rayon cord wiring or decorate a table top. Shade material of stretch velour, $140-180.

George Kovacs Lighting, Inc.
Lanky Lamp™ is a petite little delight. Pewter with "superball" feet, flame-retardant hair. 11" x 6", $95

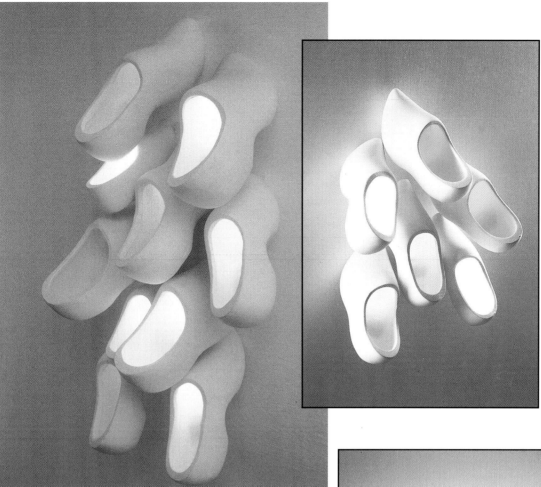

Marre Moerel
A native of Holland, Marre Moerel drew upon her Dutch roots for "Blue Moon" and "Palette of Seduction," ceramic wall hangings/floor lamps with low-voltage lights. Limited editions of five. Individual clog lights are available.
Moon: 12" x 12" x 12", $600.
Palette: 30" x 18" x 9", $1,700.

Penta SRL
Table lamp with laquered metal base and opaline blown glass, available in white, butter, amber (shown), and stained amber. 18" tall.

Katsu
These playful sculptural wall lamps were hand-crafted from aluminum sheet and detailed using a wealth of materials including Plexiglas, vinyl, and paint. Sizes range from 9-28 inches and each comes ready to hang with an 8-foot cord, $150-300.

Penta SRL
Matching floor and table lamps show off a stylish, satin poli-carbonated lampshade, available in white, ivory, green, orange, blue, and brown. The base is laquered metal. Floor lamps, 6' and 5', table lamp, 2'.

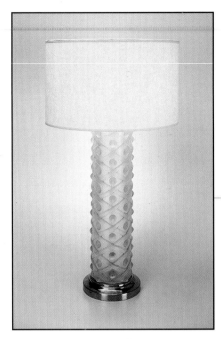

Sirmos
"Borghese" table lamp with base of CyTron®, a glass-like synthetic. Here a distinctive geometric patern gives this table lamp a retro twist that is both classic and current. 16.5" x 16.5" x 10", $1,444.

Penta SRL
A luminuos column, this floor lamp comes in satin or embossed, dull nickel, with solid cherry or wengè. The diffuser of blown opaline glass is available in white, amber, green, and blue. 6' tall.

David Howell & Company
This lighting fixtures begs to be touched, with marbles that glow and grow warm and roll within their grid when stroked. Available in seven different shades, or custom color combinations. 5" diameter. $175.

George Kovacs Lighting, Inc.
Like a nest harboring an antennaed creature, this wall sconce was designed by Dennis Higgins. 20" x 14", $160.

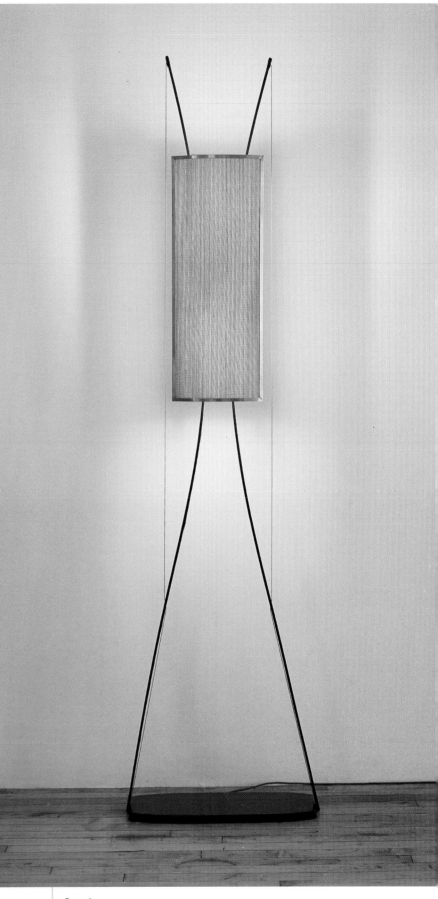

Cotule
Rising from a flat base, this floor lamp sways slightly when air moves around it. The combination of motion and the iridescent moray pattern created by the molded stainless steel mesh shade makes the piece seem alive. 72" x 10", $1,800.

Spaced Out
Called Snap lights in the United
States, these lamps are made by two
interlocking 3mm folded perspex
pieces. Designed by Zach Pulman
and James Engel, the lights can be
hung, stacked, or interlocked.
Approximately 3.5" x 3.5" x 8.25".

Michel Harvey Cèramique Inc
In imitation of real-life paper and cloth, creator Michel Harvey uses ceramics to create these unique lighting units. Bag, 7" x 5" x 13", $90.

Archaic Smile, Inc.
A hand-pinstriped steel base is topped by a silkscreen decorated shade in "Flame Job." 21" tall, $84.

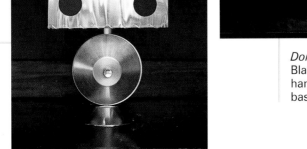

Donovan Design
"Mr. Lucky" table lamp with moiré shade is 15.75" tall with center-mounted on/off switch, $400.

Donovan Design
Black and white table lamp with hand-painted shade on solid maple base. 20" x 13" diameter, $650.

Light Ray Studios Inc.
Architect Rae Douglas designed this "Feather Cloud" mobile chandelier to create a subtle and ever-changing display of light and shadow. Available in a variety of materials and finishes, and in sizes that work with a standard 8' ceiling up to monumental size. Shown installed at a residence in Maui, Hawaii, $4,500.

Light Ray Studios Inc.
A sconce designed to complement the Feather Cloud mobile chandelier. 24" tall with a 4" projection, $600.

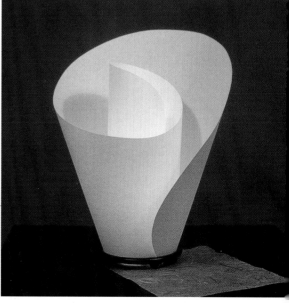

Zumaluma, Inc.
A refreshing "Lily" by designer Elsie Crawford. A related lily sconce was given *Design Journal's* "Best of L.A. Designweek Award" in 1999. 13" x 14" x 10". $180.

Light Ray Studios Inc.
This wall sconce projects rainbow light patterns onto its immediate wall surface. The fixture's reflective disk can be tilted, warped, or cut into standard or custom shapes to create a variety of lighting effects, turning a wall into a rich tapestry of light and color. Available in a variety of metal finishes. 4-8" x 3" wall projection, $100-200 depending on reflector shape.

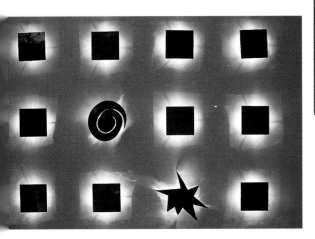

Light Ray Studios Inc.
This mobile chandelier projects a rich amber glow. Rae Douglas designed "Fire Wand" in the arts and crafts tradition, with an eye toward standard 8-foot ceilings. Installed at a residence in Berkeley, California. 12" x 48" diameter, $1,500.

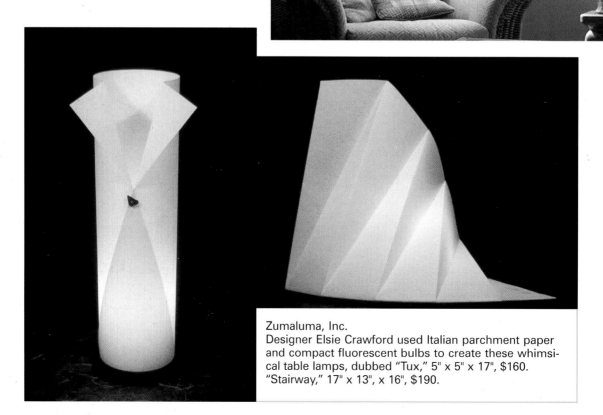

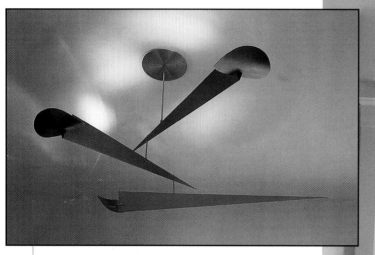

Light Ray Studios Inc.
The "Apollo 2000" chandelier projects multi-colored spectral light patterns onto its immediate surroundings. The color-anodized titanium body also changes color when viewed from different angles. 12" x 48", $3,600.

Zumaluma, Inc.
Designer Elsie Crawford used Italian parchment paper and compact fluorescent bulbs to create these whimsical table lamps, dubbed "Tux," 5" x 5" x 17", $160. "Stairway," 17" x 13", x 16", $190.

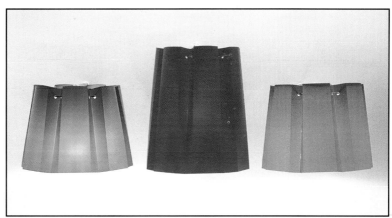

Bone Simple Design Colorful wall sconces from the Flexion Series are made of polypropylene. Small: 11" x 9", $90. Large: 11" x 12", $96.

Pearce S. Lashmett "Astros" fluorescent acrylic rings are sandwiched between chrome-plated steel disks and mounted on a wire base for a space station effect. 9" x 9" x 10.5", $365.

Pearce S. Lashmett Punctuated vinyl is used to create a durable bag light, "Mack Lamp," lit by a compact fluorescent bulb. 8" x 4" x 10", $175.

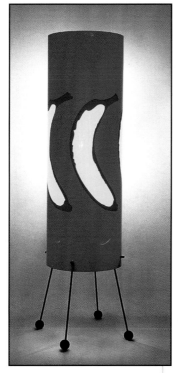

Yayo! Designs, Inc. Decorative plastic tubes top wire base for a simplistic fixture that makes a bold statement with over 24 different designs. 20" x 5.5", $49.

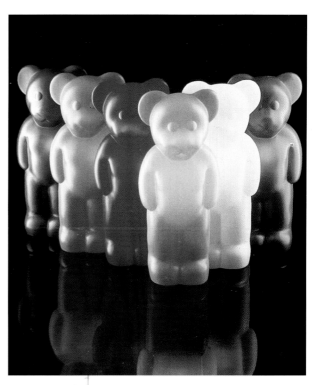

Yayo! Designs, Inc. "Lumibär" light, designed for indoor and outdoor use, available in a bold, basic color palette. 23" tall, $110.

47

Dez Ryan Studio
Two diminutive table lamps stretch their silken shades incongruously above hand-turned and painted wooden necks and hand-blown glass bulb bodies. "Amber," 24", $590.
"Polka," 25", $790.

Dez Ryan Studio
"Mrs. Wallflower" sconce with hand-blown glass body. 20" tall, $900.

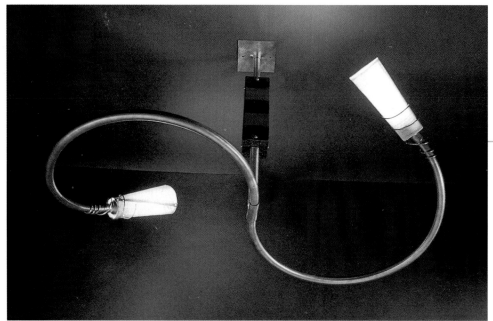

Fire & Water Lighting
Dimmable compact fluorescent lighting is the technological key behind this graceful design. This two-bulb ceiling fixture is available in custom designs and finishes. 40" x 23" x 16", $1,020.

Harry Allen & Associates
"Rubber Lamp" with layered colors. 11.5" x 4" x 4", $480.

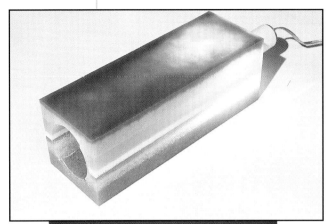

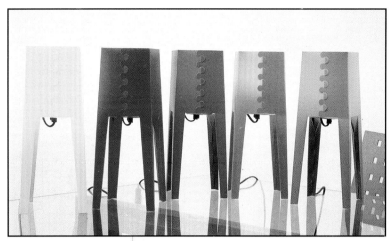

Alva
Table lamp with interlocking front makes a colorful statement. 13" tall, $38.

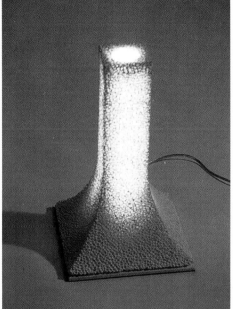

Harry Allen & Associates
"Table Tower" of ceramic foam. 13.5" x 8". Not currently in production.

Harry Allen & Associates
The "Plato Lamp" seems to dance on the floor while casting colorful shadows. Crafted from steel, plastic, and expanded metal. 21" x 19" x 17", $460.

FANTASY & ROMANCE

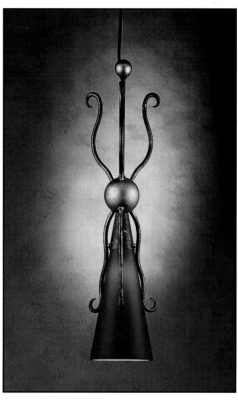

George Kovacs Lighting, Inc
ABOVE: "Chateau Moderne" chandelier supports geometric diffusers in white or blue. Finish in antique black, gold leaf, or silver leaf chip. 24" x 20", $1,125.

ABOVE: RIGHT:
Primitive pendant with blue shade (also available in white). 23" x 5.5" shade, $685.

RIGHT:
A "Bonfire" of twigs surround this 25-watt candelabra designed by Lights Up. 20" x 5", $150.

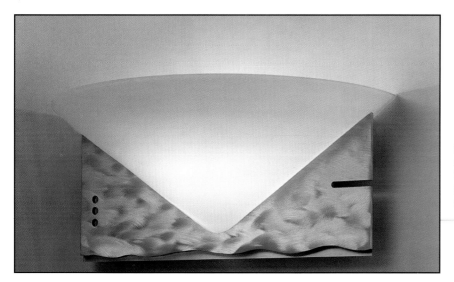

George Kovacs Lighting, Inc.
A shell of satin opal glass floats in a sea of disc-finished aluminum with burnished brass detail. 6.5" x 15.5" x 8", $685.

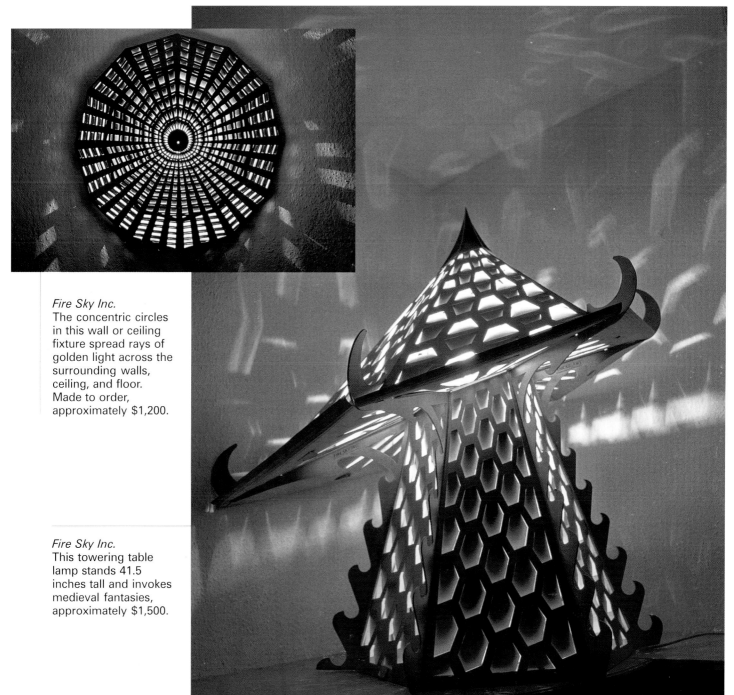

Fire Sky Inc.
The concentric circles in this wall or ceiling fixture spread rays of golden light across the surrounding walls, ceiling, and floor. Made to order, approximately $1,200.

Fire Sky Inc.
This towering table lamp stands 41.5 inches tall and invokes medieval fantasies, approximately $1,500.

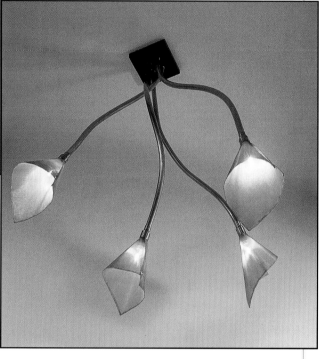

Fire & Water Lighting
The Calla Lily Series fixtures are made of copper tubing with metal mesh shades in copper and/or brass and are available in custom designs and special finishes. The bases and other parts are made from a composite of recycled paper and soy flour, a material with the look of granite, along with a natural oil finish, rag-applied to reduce environmental hazards. Floor lamp, 79" x 22" x 14", $995.
Table lamp, 28" x 14" x 8", $525.
Ceiling fixture, 26" x 36", $1,100.
Two-light wall sconce, 28" x 14" x 5", $485.
Three-light sconce, 15" x 20" x 10", $692.

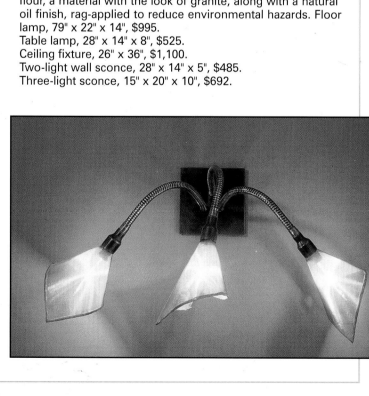

Aqua Creations
The whimsical looking "Starlights" are available in three sizes, ranging from 19 to 80 inches in length. These fixtures were designed to cling to either ceiling or wall, $1,400-2,300.

Aqua Creations
The shell-like "Coral" fixture evokes a glowing, underwater organism that is at home either on walls or ceilings. It is available in three sizes, ranging from 19 to 28 inches in length, $1,300-1,600.

Aqua Creations
"Aqua Lily 2" and "Aqua Lily 3" floor lamps stand almost 6 feet tall and cast a warm glow. The shades were crafted of silk on metal, the bases of hand-sculpted sawdust and epoxy on wood, $4,700.

Dez Ryan Studio
"Tina Tina" lamp with handblown glass orbs and hand-sewn silk shade watercolored in jungle hues. 30" tall, $1,500.

Dez Ryan Studio
Designer Dez Ryan calls her lamp shades "wonked out." Here are two colorful examples, "Kenya" and "Conga." 34" tall, $1,450.

Jezebel, Inc.
Handmade glass lamps feature a wrought iron base with a natural iron or oxidized patina finish, crowned by a hand-rolled and slumped stained glass shade. 17" tall, $220.

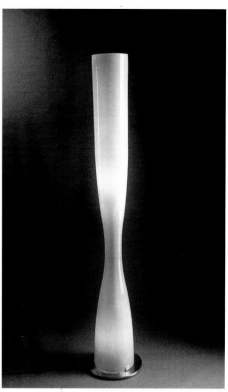

Andromeda
"Aega Terra" — A towering tube of glass, available in white, amber, grey, and blue, stretches 1.83 meters tall, $2,600.

Andromeda
"Roxie's Mod-Louis" — Bicarbonate of soda is the secret to the tiny bubbles in this festive, handmade chandelier, $2,480.

Resolute
The Paper Lights Collection utilizes diffusers made from calendered aramid fiber or aramid/mylar composites — offering the warm glow of parchment paper with high heat resistance. Durable and can be cleaned with household cleaners. "Helen Ceiling," 21" x 18.75", $400. "Helen Wall," 9" x 11", $130.

Emily McLennan
Floor lamps of turned wood with paper shade, available in 57", 62", and 65" heights, custom made in a variety of woods and finishes. Starting at $2,393.

Penta SRL
A wooden floor lamp, available in cherry, wengè, or walnut arches gracefully to a parchment shade. 6'5" x 4.5'.

Emily McLennan
Assorted table lamps by designer Emily McLennan. "Nina," 26". "Maud," 34". "Pearl," 38". Starting at $1,040.

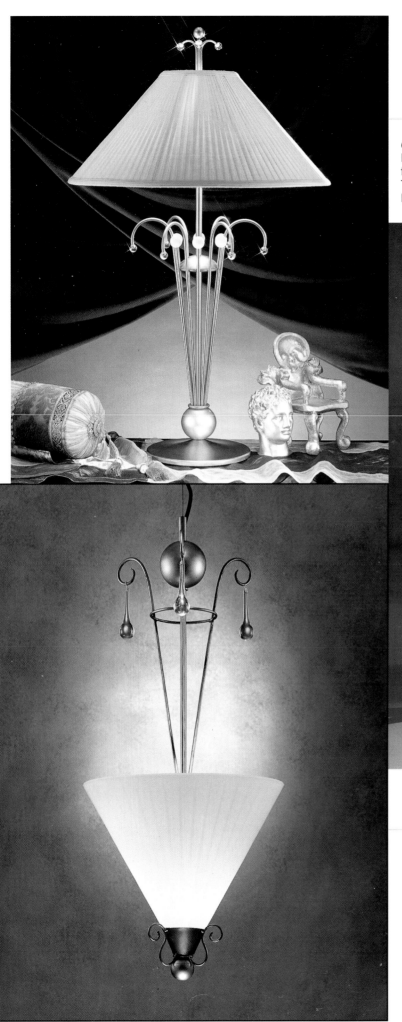

George Kovacs Lighting, Inc.
Fantasy lamps sparkle with glass beads and sparkling finishes called "golden goddess" or "silver screen." Table lamp: 35" x 22" French pleated shade, $935. Floor lamp: 72" x 12" base, $735.

George Kovacs Lighting, Inc.
A glass shade points up at a ceiling fixture that strains both up and down, movement punctuated by dangling pendants. Available in antique black chip and gold or silver leaf chip. 28" with 12.5" shade, $685.

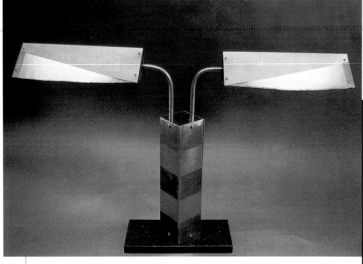

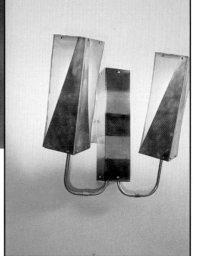

Fire & Water Lighting
The cutting-edge energy-conserving technology of dimmable compact fluorescents is teamed with decorative design in the Energia II series. The slightly tapered brass mesh diffusers enclose high-output compact fluorescents.
Table lamp, 28" x 5" x 18", $985.
Wall sconce, 16" x 15" x 4", $865.

Sirmos
ABOVE: The "Esprit" wall sconce softens light through a floral pattern etched in CyTron®, a glass-imitating synthetic. 17" x 8" x 4", $840.

RIGHT: Strict modern geometry of design on the "Treadwell" pendant is textured by a natural, organic pattern etched into the glass-like CyTron® synthetic shade. 27" x 7" x 30", $2,184.

George Kovacs Lighting, Inc.
Silk-topped table lamps with fanciful pull chains were designed by Rachel Simon. 23" x 4", $185.

Kevin Mills
This wall sconce, dubbed "Three Days," was fashioned from perforated acid-washed brass and film transparencies. 6" x 14", $630.

George Kovacs Lighting, Inc.
The "Angel" design by Dawn Ladd and Rachel Simon comes in three sizes. Floor, 56" x 9", $275. Table, 30" x 9", $235. Buffet, 21" x 5", $150.

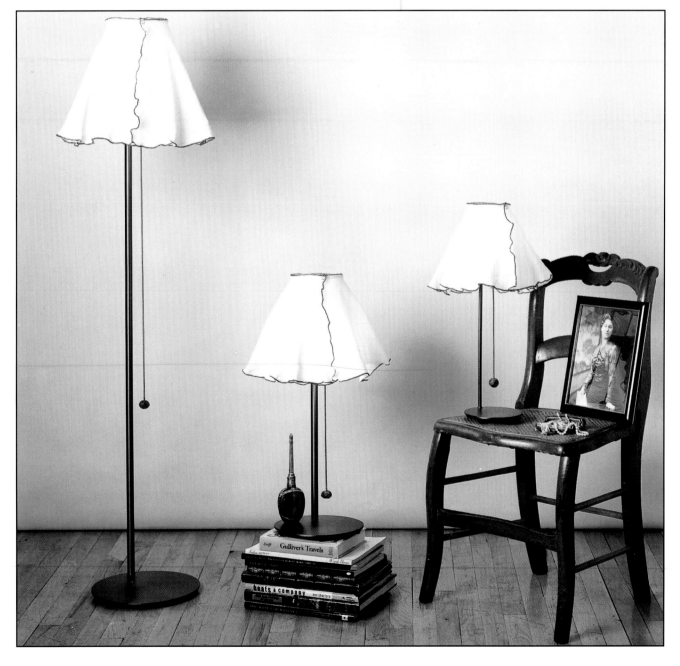

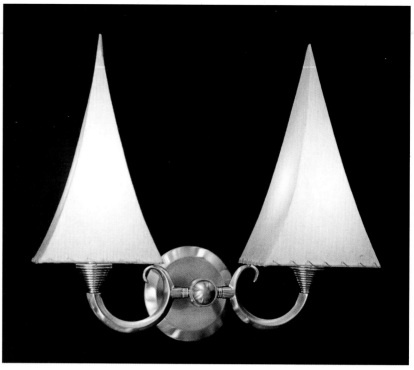

Donovan Design "Tuxedo" table lamp and double wall sconce, available in satin nickel or satin enamel bronze. Lamp, 27" x 16.75", $1,500. Sconce, 16.75" x 17", $460.

Schonbek Worldwide Lighting Ornate arms and scrolls were painstakingly cast by hand for "La Scala." The variety of handcut crystal shapes hark back to sixteenth-century chandeliers, which were hung with irregular rock crystal. 28" x 45" long, $6,750.

Schonbek Worldwide Lighting
The focal point of this lofty, modern foyer is "Trilliane," a
contemporary crystal chandelier custom-made to extra-
large dimensions. 48" x 52" long, $54,000.

Sculture in Luce
Silk and cotton paper with vegetable dyes form the intriguing wings of this butterfly lamp, suspended on copper tubing and wire. 26" tall, $185.

Sculture in Luce
The sun, in a stunning array of copper wire and vegetally-dyed silk-cotton paper, forms a foreground for this lamp. 19" tall.

Sculture in Luce
Dubbed "Eros," this bright bud of red and yellow paper on a copper frame stands 26" tall, $190.

Sculture in Luce
A flame of silk-cotton paper and copper wire bursts from a cast metal frame. 10" x 20", $205.

Sculture in Luce
A stone supports a flame-like flower of silk-cotton paper towering 22" tall, $220.

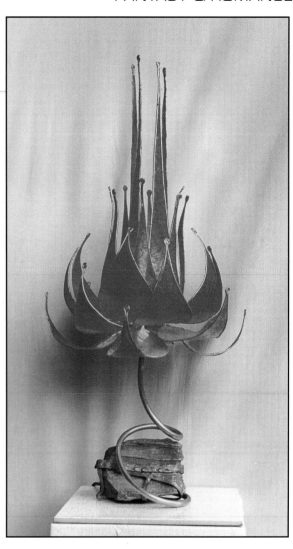

Sculture in Luce
An elfish splash of color formed by naturally dyed silk-cotton paper and blue murano beads crowns a natural sculpture of river stones and root. 32" x 13", $420.

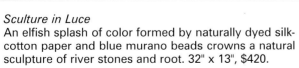

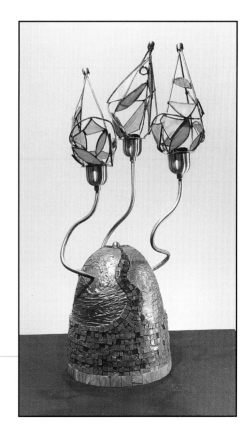

Fantarte
A helmet-like brass and mosaic base supports three whimsical shades of tiffany. 12" tall, $310.

FontanaArte USA
Small, medium, and extra-large versions of the "D. Puppa" lamp, ranging from 11"-21", $430-1,330.

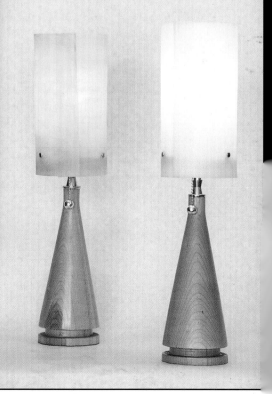

Christopher Poehlmann Studio, Inc.
Post consumer acrylic shades in white or parchment top a hand-turned maple base. No two are quite alike. 19" x 4", $370.

Trout Studios™
Broad yet delicate curves were crafted into this Baltic birch lamp base, topped by a cylindrical styrene shade. 18" x 7", $225.

Aqua Creations
Two dramatic floor lamps mimic organic images in this striking photo by Albi Serfaty. "Horn" seems precariously balanced on a small base. 51" tall, $1,900.
A group of five "Morning Glory" floor lamps glow below. 75-85" tall, $3,675.

Aqua Creations
Two wall sconces — "Candy" and "Onion" — appeal to different tastes. Candy, 14" long, $515. Onion, 35", $1,000.

Wish Designs
A bouquet of natural hickory branches is punctuated by light in this whimsical chandelier designed by Deanna Wish. 32" x 36", $790

A.E. Jennings Designs
Cactus flower "Photo Vellum"
lamp of stainless steel with handstitched shade. 8.5" x 19" tall,
$186.

Trout Studios™
A series of disks in graduating
scale animate this lamp, dubbed
"Lülu" and topped with a cylindrical styrene shade. 18" x 7", $225.

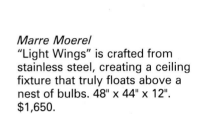

Marre Moerel
"Light Wings" is crafted from stainless steel, creating a ceiling fixture that truly floats above a nest of bulbs. 48" x 44" x 12". $1,650.

Marre Moerel
A delicate wall unit of stainless steel feathers, illuminated by a single candle-shaped incandescent bulb. 8" x 34" x 12". $475, limited edition of five.

Harry Allen & Associates "String Ball Lamps" from the Natural and Unnatural Collections crafted from twine, feathers, and epoxy. 12" x 36". Not currently in production.

Bone Simple Design
"The Beetle" sconce relies on a simplistic design of steel wire to project interesting and beautiful images found in nature, here with the image of a dragonfly. 12" x 12", $80.

Reed Bros.
BELOW LEFT: Large "Cotati Lamp" with squirrel motif, hand carved from pine. 13" x 10" x 22", $645.

BELOW RIGHT: "Cotati Chandelier" with squirrel and quail finials, hand carved from pine. 29" x 35", $3,515.

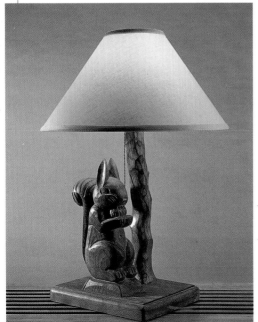

Reed Bros.
Custom-designed,
carved chandelier.
Call for a quote.

Chista
RIGHT: "Coco and Coco" —
A solid base of coconut
tree trunk supports a shade
of leather and iron. Stands
between 5.5' and 6' tall.
$800-1,000.

FAR RIGHT: A metal
structure in these "Triangle
Paper Lamps" gives
contrast to handmade
paper by New York artist
Amanda Guest. The paper
is inlaid with nails or
thread, and created
exclusively for this use.
With brass reinforcements
and foot dimmers on
medium and large models.
Range from 18" to 6' tall.
$200-400 for small and
medium models.

ACODNFKOSDFK ODFSNOK

Chista
RIGHT: "Black Coconut Monotype Lamp" — Handmade lamp features a base blackened with different pigment oils and waxes to create a rich surface. The shade is a collage of monotype prints of the designer, Alon Langotsky's, own painted works. 5' to 6' tall, by special order, $800-1,000.

FAR RIGHT: Designers Bona Maggi and Alon Langotsky were inspired by a Dayak shield from Borneo when they created this sconce, crafted from buffalo hide and bamboo. 40" x 10". $630.

Chista
A solid coconut wood base supports a leather shade. Ranging in height from 22" to 26" inches, $150-900.

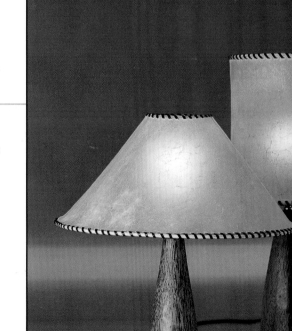

Chista
A coconut wood base supports a seaweed
shade, towering 5.5' to 6' tall. $200-800.

Mark Lee Lighting
"Zen Water Bowl" of rice
paper on a metal frame.
20" x 20" x 12", $660.

Mark Lee Lighting
"Porcelain" table lamp of rice paper.
24" x 19" x 23", $660.

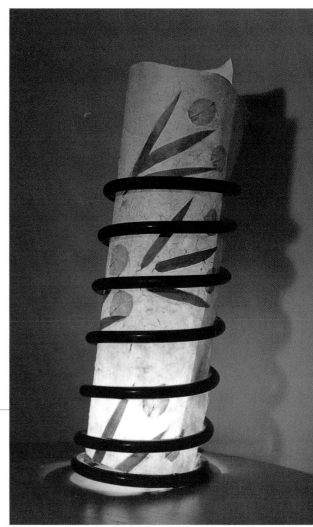

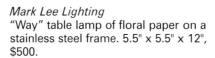

Mark Lee Lighting
"Way" table lamp of floral paper on a
stainless steel frame. 5.5" x 5.5" x 12",
$500.

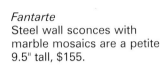

Fantarte
Steel wall sconces with marble mosaics are a petite 9.5" tall, $155.

George Kovacs Lighting, Inc.
Squat table lamps in smoked steel or copper penny can accommodate up to 150 watts. 18" x 17", $185.

INTO THE FUTURE

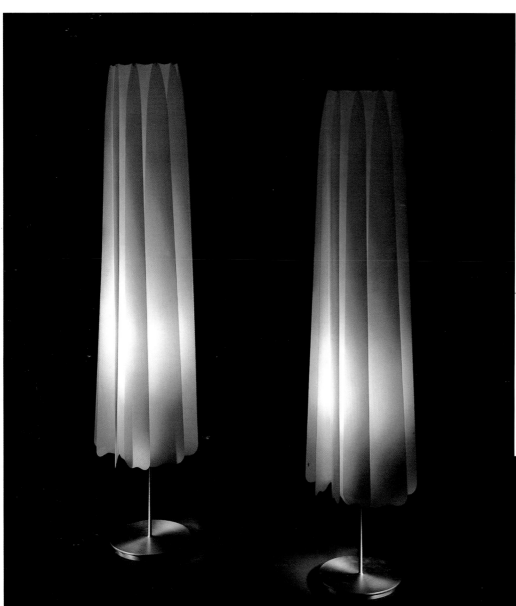

LEFT & OPPOSITE:
George Kovacs Lighting, Inc.
Designed by Alecia Wesner,
these satin steel finished
bases support the translucent
petals of ". Space Boy table
lamp, 21" x 6", $275.
Floor lamp, 51" x 9", $435.
Pendant, 9" x 6", $275.

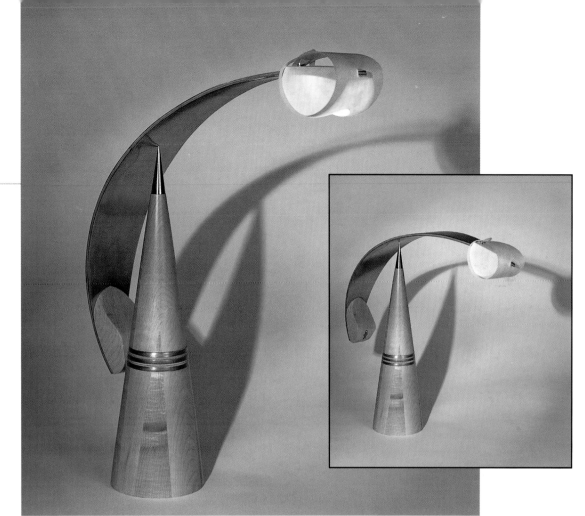

Korpon Leopairote
The designer was inspired by an exotic, fruit seed-balancing toy he played with during his childhood in Thailand. The stem balances on a single point of contact with the conical maple base and bobs with a subtle, rhythmic movement. To switch it on, the low end of the lamp is tilted down where it is magnetically connected to the cone, causing the light to go on. 17" x 14.5", $1,200.

Daniel Schreiber
Pink, luminous sculpture chandelier of hand-blown glass. 30" in diameter, $2,500.

Daniel Schreiber
Blue pendant lamp of hand-blown glass. 14" tall. $900.

Donovan Design
"Sir Duke II" table lamp with double moiré shade, 29" x 16", $1,500.

Ochre
Hand-blown glass "Cherub" and "Cherubino" lamps available in clear, amethyst, and grey, with wild silk shades in taupe or frost (shown). Sizes vary as each one is hand blown. Large, 27", $560. Small, 11", $380.

Donovan Design
"Royale Palm" wall sconce, 18.75" x 7", $460.
"Mrs. Ippi" lamp with double moiré shade, 24" x 8", $680.

Donovan Design
"Marcantel Cigar Table" of handwoven oak veneer
with an illuminated cylinder in the solid steel base.
20" diameter top, 24" tall, $1,600; 31" tall, $2,300.

Donovan Design
"Baby Bruno" wall sconce can
be mounted up or down.
Matching table lamp available.
9.25" x 8", $350.

Donovan Design
"Piaf" wall
sconce has
sandblasted
glass column
with a white
liner in satin
nickel or enamel
bronze on steel.
12" x 5", $365.

Donovan Design
"Amadeus" table lamp has a hand-formed shade over solid maple base with brass detailing. 25.5" x 15.5" x 6", $650.

Fantarte
A double table lamp of burnished brass and tiffany glass creates a floral effect. 21" tall, $115.

Fantarte
A steel table lamp with tiffany glass in a mosaic shade. 17" tall, $93.

Fantarte
A tiffany glass shade tops a floor lamp of burnished brass. 14" x 4.5', $185.

Estiluz
Suspension ceiling fixture provides direct and indirect lighting with rectangular diffuser with satin glass and anti-dazzling metal grid. Steel with gold-plated, chrome, and black lacquer finishes. Designed by Leonardo Marelli. Approximately 42-21" x 24". $475-650.

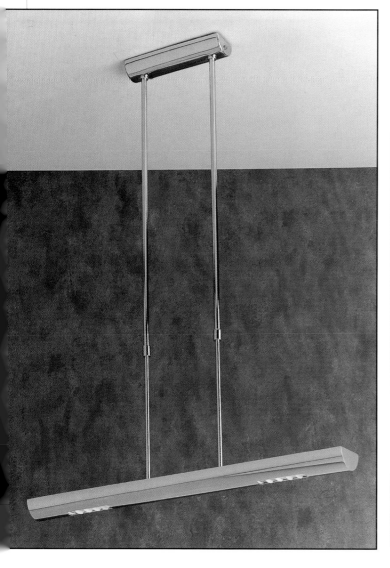

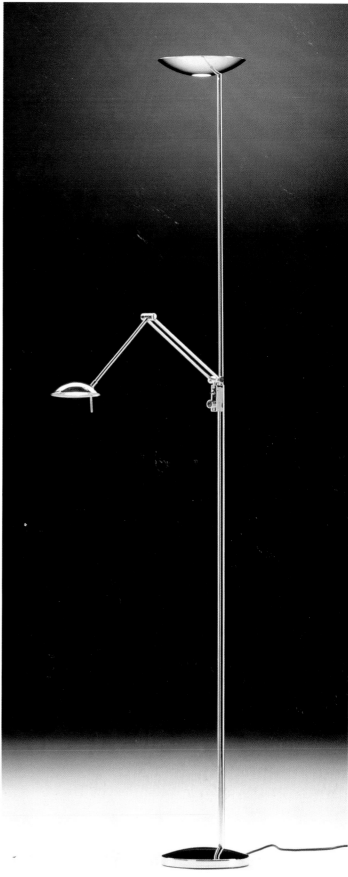

Estiluz
Perfect for mood lighting or serious reading, this halogen lamp has a built-in dimmer. Adjustable head extends 26.75" from the base. Designed by Leonardo Marelli. Available in gold-plate, chrome, and black lacquer finishes. $770-975.

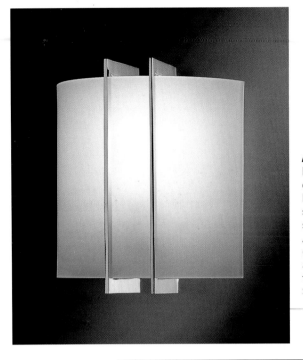

Estiluz Incandescent wall lamp with satin glass shade. Available in gold-plate and chrome finishes. $365.

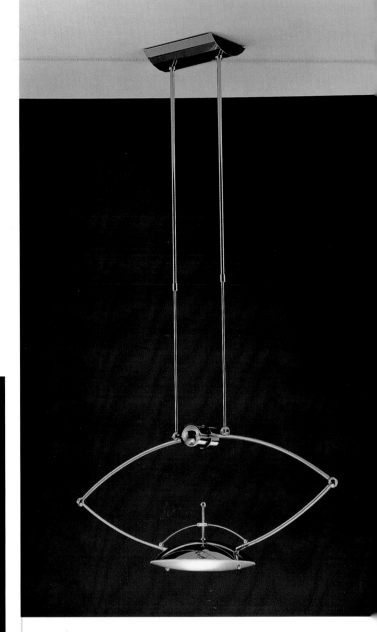

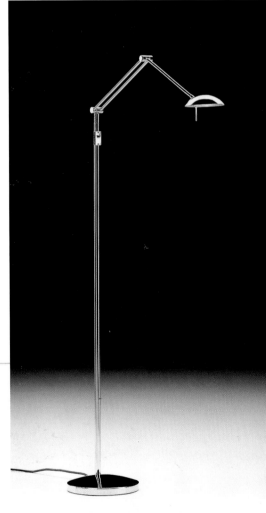

Reading lamp stands 41" from the floor, with an arm that extends 23". Available in gold-plate, chrome, and black lacquer. $590-745.

Estiluz
ABOVE: Ceiling fixture has telescopic ability to provide direct lighting with halogen lamp through satin glass. Extends from approximately 21" to 42". A favorite with architects. $1,170.

Estiluz
BELOW: Halogen table lamp extends 21" x 14" tall. Hi-low switch. Available in gold-plate, chrome, or black lacquer. $535-455.

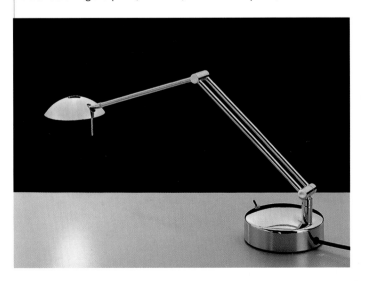

Estiluz
Suspension lamp telescopes horizontally from 29.5" to 49.25", providing direct and indirect lighting through satin opal glass. Available in gold-plate, chrome, black, and white finishes. Also available with blue glass. $825-1,015.

Estiluz
Halogen ceiling lamp with glass diffuser, available in widths from 8.25", 12.5", and 16", with gold, chrome, black, and white finishes. $230-330.

Estiluz
Halogen sconce provides indirect lighting and extends 6" inches from the wall. $215-265.

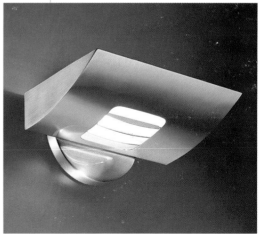

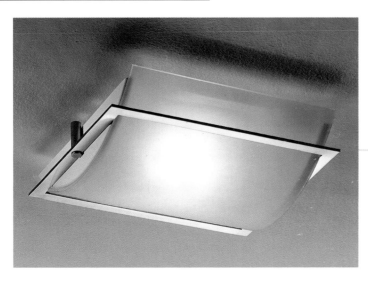

Estiluz
Celing lamp uses halogen and a satin glass diffuser to provide direct and indirect lighting. Available in gold, chrome, nickel, and black. $460.

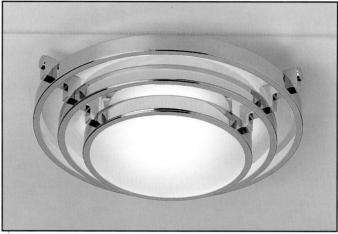

Estiluz
Hallogen wall lamp provides direct and indirect lighting with satin glass, gold, chrome, nickel, and black finishes. $260.

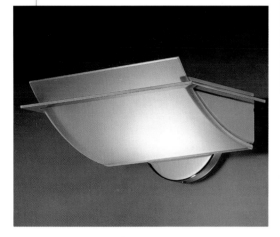

Estiluz
Circular diffuser and satin glass ad character to this round ceiling fixture designed by Leonardo Marelli. Available in gold-plate, chrome, and white. $250-310.

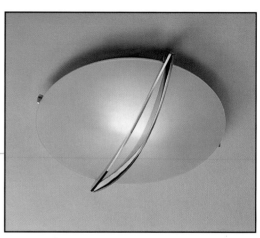

Estiluz
Halogen ceiling lamp with satin glass diffuser, available in gold, chrome, black, and white. $260-370.

George Kovacs Lighting, Inc.
A grid of satin steel lined with white parchment diffuser creates a bright, geometric candelabra fixture. 20.5", $160.
Matching sconce, 17"H, $485.

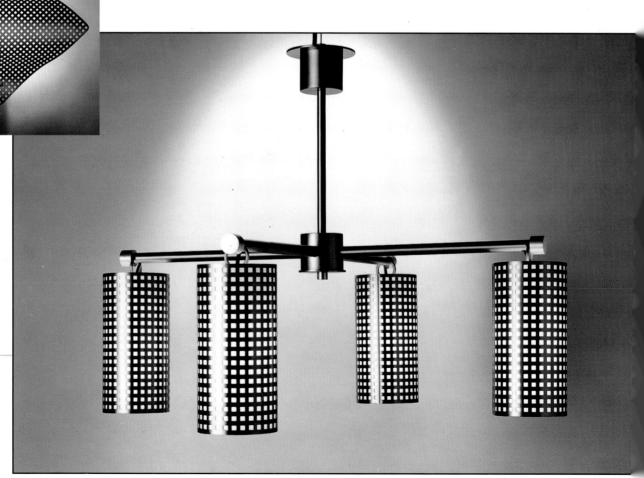

Kevin Mills
"Turbulina" was fashioned from a jet engine turbine equipped with incandescent lights. It can be mounted on the ceiling. 36" x 30", $4,500.

Lush Life
Floor lamp of powder-coated steel and nickelplated beadchain projects a burst of halogen lighting. 75" x 18", $1,200.

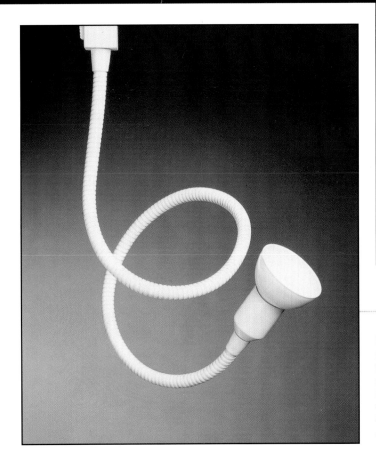

W.A.C. Lighting
Flexible swivel lamp includes a miniature track that can be customized for installation on or off the ceiling or wall or regressed for a built-in look. Available in black and white finishes, with lamps ranging from 20 to 50 watts. Maximum extension of 18", $35.

W.A.C. Lighting
Low-voltage glass and metal pendant ceiling fixtures
come in a range of glass colors including red, yellow,
white, blue, green, seafoam, and pink, as well as in gold
and brushed-aluminum metal finishes. Pendants can be
attached to a track. Suspension cords come in 48- and
96-inch lengths, $80 with wiring components.

FLOS USA Inc.
The "Glo-Ball" of blown opal white glass softens
and spreads a glow over a large area. It is
available in table, floor, and hanging models,
with diffuser diameters of 13-17.5", $450-1,115.

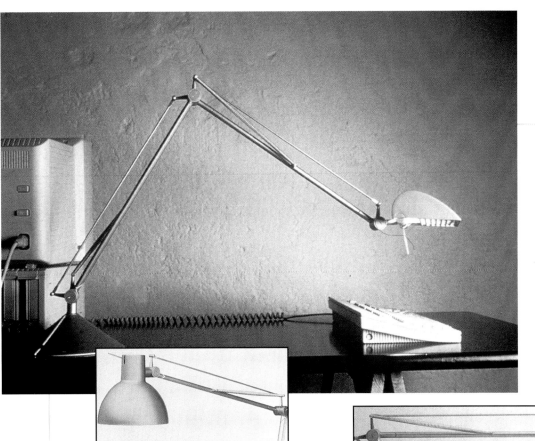

FLOS USA Inc.
This "Archimoon" fixture does multi-tasking. Fitted for four distinct shades, the lamps adjustable, spring-balanced tubular arms help keep the shade horizontal to work surfaces, eliminating glare. Full extension is approximately 34-39" depending on the shades. Shade options shown are Eco, Classic, Tech, and Soft, $295-395.

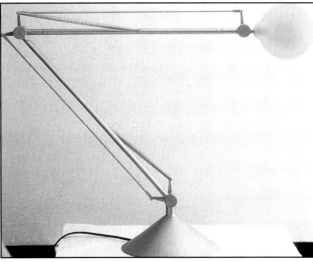

Fire & Water Lighting
The "MR16 Series" was named for the bulbs they prominently employ. The delicate shape of the bulb's reflector is made an integral part of the design by placing the exposed bulbs at the ends of copper tubes.
Four-way sconce, 7" x 7" x 8", $640.
Helix floor lamp, 67" x 14", $700.
Four-bulb pendant, 56" x 24", $815.

FLOS USA Inc.
The "Romeo Moon" diffuser is a translucent fluted shade of pressed glass that spreads light over a large area. The inner egg-shaped glass diffuser has been etched to soften the harsh look of a bare lamp and provide even light distribution on a horizontal surface. Table lamps come in 25.6" and 28.7" heights with shade diameters of 13" and 19.5", $695-995. Suspension fixtures are available with 13.4" and 19.7" diameters. $535-595.

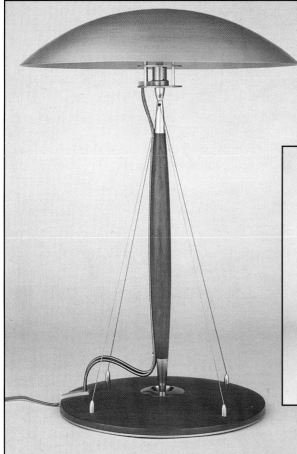

Prisco Studio
A tension-supported articulating desk lamp with dimmer switch comes in a table-top version (shown) and floor lamp. Crafted from cherry with anodized aluminum and stainless steel. 19" x 25", $3,000.

Manic Creative Art & Design
Designer Beth Weintraub uses delicately etched zinc material to create her lighting. The "Whorl" pendant is so light it can hang from its own cord. 16" x 8". $315. "Bamboo" torchiere: 25" x 8". $495. "Twist" floor lamp: 78" x 11". $798.

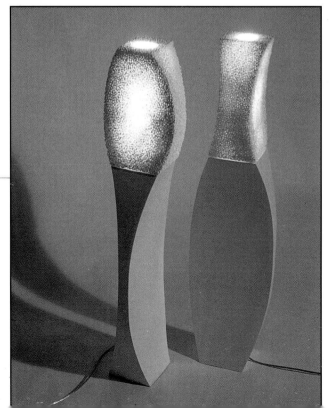

Harry Allen & Associates
The complimentary sculptural forms of two "Twist" lamps are capped with ceramic foam diffusers. 33" x 5". Not currently in production.

Alva
FAR LEFT: "MOO" floor lamp with conical difuser stands 63 inches tall. It was crafted from steel and polypropylene, $160.

LEFT: "LAN" table lamp with flared cone-shaped diffuser stands 18 inches tall, $50.

Alva
"PAL" space-shaped table lamp diffuses light in a warm glow. Available in a multitude of colors. 9.5" tall, $50.

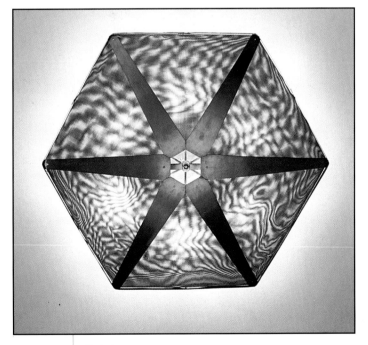

Cotule
Stainless steel "Iris" wall sconce seems to focus on the onlooker. Two sizes: 36" x 18", $1,300; 24" diameter, $1,250.

FontanaArte USA
Egg-shaped lamps in three sizes, ranging in diameter from 7"-17", $215-615.

Marre Moerel
In her Soft Box Series, artist/designer Marre Moerel experiments with soft geometrical forms in earthenware ceramic, lit from within, and ready to hang, stand, or mount on the wall. Ranging from 10-23".

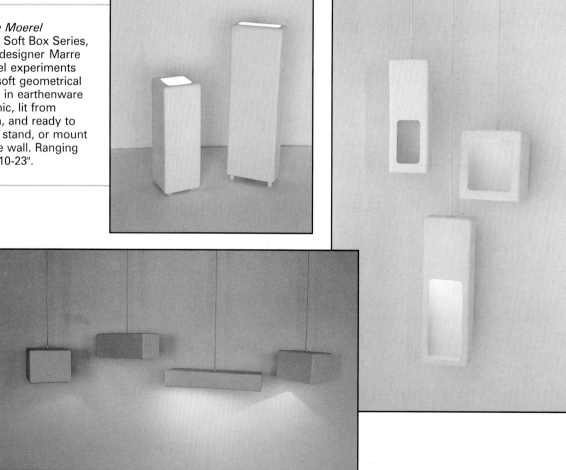

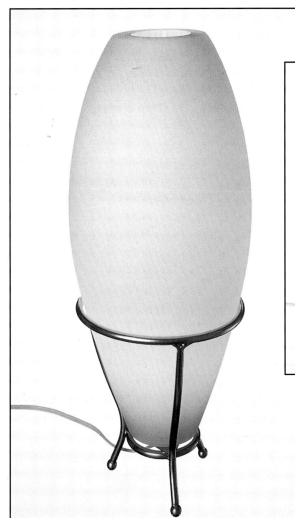

Bone Simple Design
"Egg" and "Cocoon" table lamps create a warm, soothing glow through a mouth-blown, sandblasted glass shade that nestles in a steel wire-formed stand. Cocoon: 15" x 5.5", $140. Egg: 10" x 5", $75.

Bone Simple Design
A lamp diffuses light through stacked acrylic discs. 6" x 11". $450. A polypropylene shade features an orange and white zigzag fold and nickel-plated hardware. 13" x 27.5", $420.

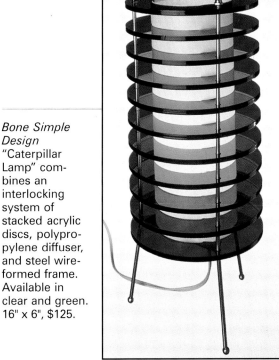

Bone Simple Design
"Caterpillar Lamp" combines an interlocking system of stacked acrylic discs, polypropylene diffuser, and steel wire-formed frame. Available in clear and green. 16" x 6", $125.

Bone Simple Design
Fluted shades of polypropylene
create a delicate look on these
table lamps from the "Cumulus"
series. Floor lamps and pendants
also available. 10" x 10", $137.
10" x 14", $150.
14" x 14", $160.

Nelson
Ceramic forms cast an other-
worldly glow in these designs by
Julie Nelson. "Sponge" light, 13" x
11", $380.
"Obelisk," 21" x 8", $440.
"Elipse," 12" x 17", $440.

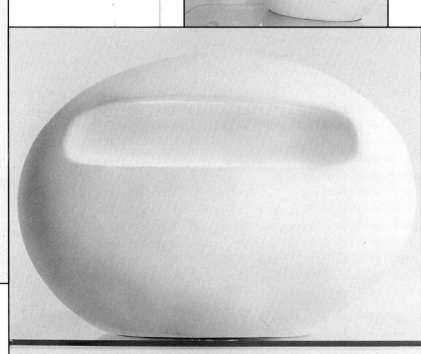

Aqua Creations
"Glowing Night Light 2" creates a deep sea fantasy in this photo by Ayala Serfaty. It is made of copper and has more than 10,000 tiny holes made with a small metal needle. 20" diameter, $6,000.

Fire & Water Lighting
The "Frankie Goes Fluorescent" series features dimmable compact fluorescent bulbs, recycled glass, and Environ™, a biocomposite of recycled and sustainable materials. Custom designs and special finishes are available. Vertical sconce, 4" x 7.5" x 13.5", $435.
Table lamp (also available in similar dimensions, with mount, for ceiling fixture), 18" x 10" x 5", $625.

Benza, Inc.
Drop Lamp and Bowl, designed by Giovanni Pellone, is made of a translucent cast resin that comes in white, orange, green, and blue. Handmade in Italy, with a 15' cord. 13.5" x 5.5".

Resolute
"The Birds," shown here in pendant and wall-mount forms, utilize the demanding process of *incalmo*, where two separate bubbles of glass are opened, matched exactly, and joined together mouth to mouth to create a single piece. "Bird Pendant," opal white and transparent aqua, 9.5" tall, $350.
"King Bird Pendant," steel gray, 16.5", $500.
Wall mount, 5" diameter, 14" tall shade, $400.

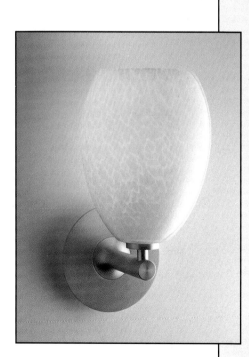

Resolute
This variegated visual texture was achieved as the glass blower rolled a hot bubble base in crushed glass, fusing a mottled coating onto the surface before blowing it out. The "Tortoise" is a mix of ambors over ivory; "Ivory" is a subtle tone of white chip on off-white ivory. Pendant: 5.75" x 7.5" with stainless steel aircraft cable that allows a drop of up to 6', $300.
Wall mount, 11" x 7". $350.

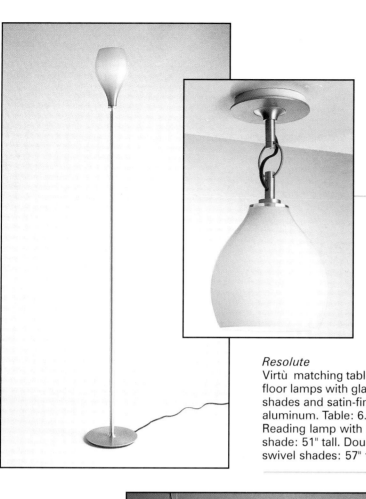

Resolute
Using a comprehensive, flexible hardware system, The Clouds series allows Design Director Douglas Varey to collaborate with the design community in creating variations in floor, ceiling, and wall-mounted fixtures. Floor: 72" x 10", $500. Ceiling, 14", $350.

Resolute
Virtù matching table and floor lamps with glass shades and satin-finished aluminum. Table: 6.5" tall. Reading lamp with swivel shade: 51" tall. Double swivel shades: 57" tall.

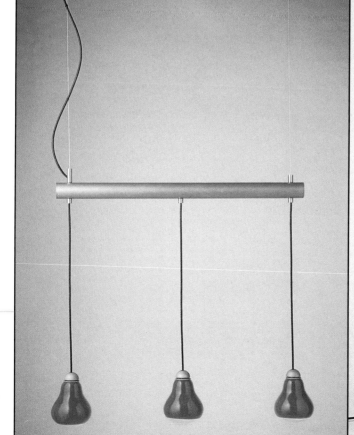

Resolute
"Triple Ben Pendant with hand-blown glass shades and aluminum. 29" from tube to bottom of glass, $900.

Resolute
"Symphony Pendant" fixture has brushed clear anodized aluminum reflector and shade with aramid/ mylar composite diffusers. 36" diameter.

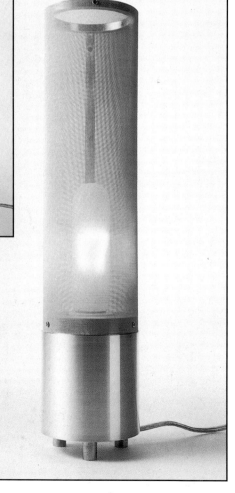

biproduct
Stacking floor lamp shown with variation of rings of aluminum, powder-coated aluminum, and stainless steel mesh. 5" x 33", $450.

biproduct
Stacking table lamp, with detachable rings of aluminum, powder-coated aluminum, and stainless steel mesh. 6" x 16", $275.

Light Ray Studios Inc.
This mobile chandelier was designed for a triangular atrium. The three-sided shape is reflected in the shapes of the fins and in the light baffles above each cone, which are made of interlocking triangles and utilize spectral lighting technology to reflect rainbow light to the sides and the ground while permitting the bulk of the white light to reach the ceiling. Shown installed at the Monchnik residence in Bloomfield, Michigan; 14' x 5', $10,000.

Light Ray Studios Inc.
Architect Rae Douglas was inspired by the sculptures of Alexander Calder when he created this "Spiral Eye" mobile chandelier. Each appendage orbits freely. Finishes, proportion, and the number of appendages can be varied to fit horizontal or vertical spaces. Shown installed at the Gartner residence in Maui, Hawaii; 12' x 4', $10,000.

Emily McLennan
The designer was inspired by outer space in her creation of these wall sconces, named "Lunalites." Her thought: astral bodies orbiting the planets tend to be rounded and to have female names. She casts her creations then paints them with textured milk paint to create a subtly cratered surface. Starting at $570.

Olafur Thordarson/Dingaling Studio, Inc.
"Tulip" and "Fungi" floor lamps, constructed of translucent soft resin, steel, and concrete, tower 7 feet tall. Three colors available, $3,600.

Nelson
"Orbital" table lamp diffuses light both above and below a donut shade of ceramic. 22" x 9", $360.

Nelson
"Venus backlighter" of
ceramic. 11.5" x 4", $90.

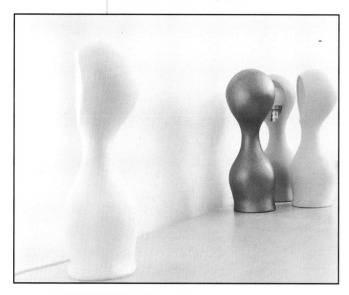

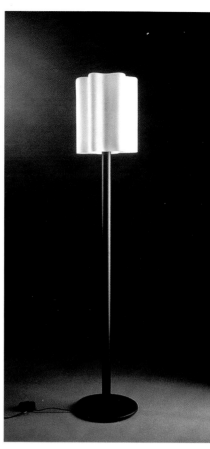

Andromeda
Fluted glass
shade of "Mod
Aqualta"
crowns a
chrome floor
lamp. 71" tall,
$1,390.

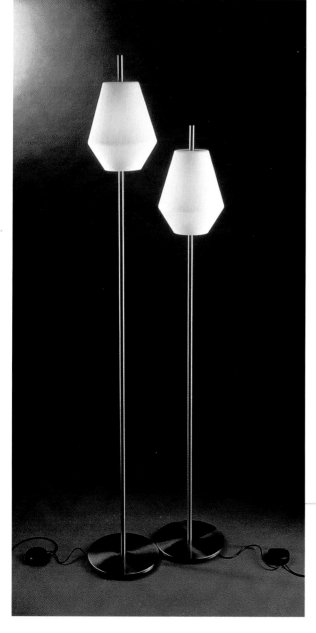

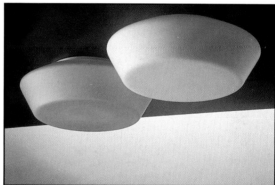

Andromeda
"Mod Farsora" glass ceiling
fixtures measure 6" x 16", $470.

Andromeda
" Mod Suri" floor lamp with glass
globe on satin chrome base. 62"
or 68" tall, $880.

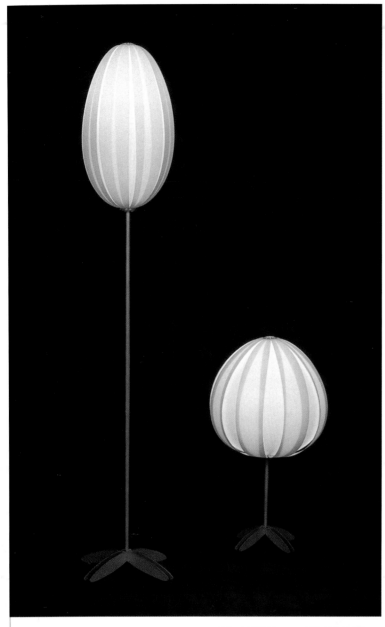

Penta SRL
A blown glass diffuser in transparent finish creates a crystal space-age effect atop a nickle base. The "Planet" shade is available in satin, acidated, and amber acidated, and the base in cherry or American walnut. 4.25" tall.

Sirmos
The "Belvedere" wall sconce takes its character from its distinctive geometric pattern, molded of colorful glass-like CyTron® synthetic. 17" x 8" x 4", $852.

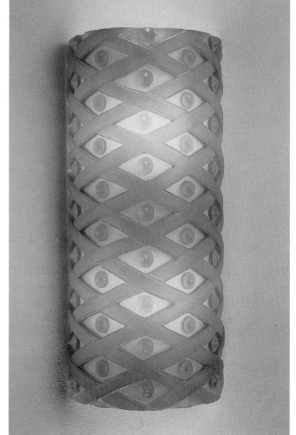

Kundalini
Named for the floral symbol of spiritual fulfilment, the "Loto" floor and table lamps' light diffuser has sixteen overlapped polycarbonate strips that are adjustable to create rounder or more elongated shapes. Now in the permanent collection of the Museum of Modern Art in New York City. Floor lamp, $400; table lamp, $380.

Penta SRL
As it's named, so it is, as this "Tower" of white satin glass stands just over 6 feet. Designed by Wanni Rondani, it is also available in blown or crackle glass, and in blue and amber hues. The base is available in cherry or American walnut.

Sirmos
Designed by company president Craig Corona, the Athenia Collection of lighting features hexagonal stems and fluted shades, with delicately curved panels for a modern look. All models are available in hand-painted steel with optional integral color shades of CyTron®, a synthetic glass-like material. "Athene" floor lamp, 64" x 20", $2,490. "Grega" table lamp, 24" x 18", $1,450-1,530.

Sirmos
The folded, frosted shades of this Magic Flute Collection imitate glass with CyTron®, a synthetic material available in thirteen standard jewel colors. "Rhapsody Table Lamp," 24" x 17", $1,830. "Sonata Pendant," 24" drop x 17", $2,370. "Prelude Wall Sconce," 6" x 17" x 7", $1,128.

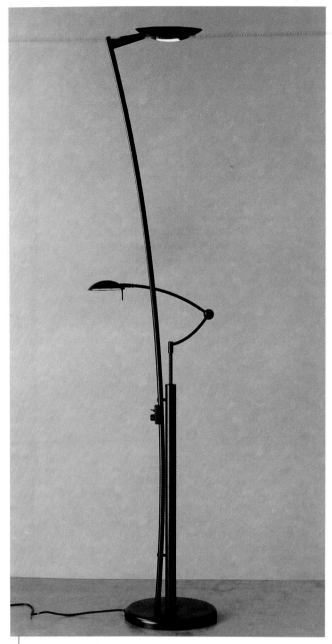

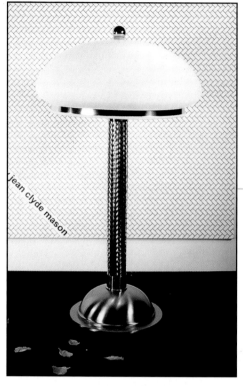

George Kovacs Lighting, Inc.
A woven steel base with brass accents makes this design by Jean Clyde Mason unique. 21" x 12" shade, $375.

George Kovacs Lighting, Inc.
Rounded and cone-shaped pendant lamps of opaque glass rest in satin steel frames with rubber details. 20-27" x 8", with 10' adjustable wire and cable, $500-625.

Estiluz
Halogen floor lamp provides direct and indirect lighting. Features an electronic dimmer, transformer, and double-intensity switch. Available in gold-plated, chrome, and black finishes. 70.5" x 26.5", $1,084-1,377.

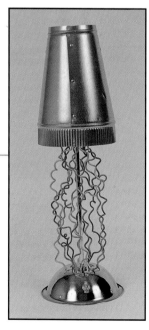

David Long
Usually hidden when they do their work, designer David Long wanted to see these vibrantly hued wires brought into the light, quite literally, so he created the "Colorful Wires Lamp" to show them off. 22" x 6" base, $195.

George Kovacs Lighting, Inc. A modern version of the hurricane lamp, this contemporary glass tube supports a satin aluminum shade and polished brass, all glowing from a halogen bulb. 18" x 17", $750.

George Kovacs Lighting, Inc. "Le Salon Grande" design by Robert Sonneman features satin brass with lacquered black stem and amber glass, or satin nickel with white opal glass. Floor lamp, 55" x 11", $1,185-1,500. Table lamp, 24" x 10", $935-1,250.

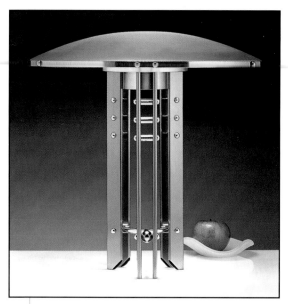

George Kovacs Lighting, Inc.
Appearing ready for takeoff, this design by Robert Sonneman comes in the satin aluminum with chrome accents design pictured, or a matte black with brass details, all topped by a mesh top with frosted glass insert. 20" x 20" shade, $1,625.

George Kovacs Lighting, Inc.
Christopher Hartmann designed this utilitarian duo of suspension cables. Table lamp, 27" x 16" dome, $310. Floor lamp, 54" x 16" dome, $375.

George Kovacs Lighting, Inc.
This double-bulb table lamp is available in the pewter with gold accents shown, and copper with gold or black with gold. 16" x 18" shade, $560.

George Kovacs Lighting, Inc. A bold copper wall sconce, also available in pewter or black, with gold accents. 9.5" x 8" glass shade, $325-350.

George Kovacs Lighting, Inc. Dawn Ladd design mimics microphone stand with space-specific spotlights. Floor lamp: 72" x 12", $560. Table lamp, 27" x 11" magnetic adjustable arm, $435.

Archaic Smile, Inc. Two floor lamps diffuse a room's worth of bright light. On the left, the "Fusion 3" features a hand-laced and printed shade. The lamp on the right is dubbed "Tiki Torch." Both stand about 5 feet tall, $180.

A.E. Jennings Designs   page 67
240 Wythe Ave.
Brooklyn, NY 11211
718-599-1204/Fax: 718-599-0203
Adrienne Jennings, company owner and designer, merges her technical and artistic accomplishments in sculpture and photography for a fine art approach to home furnishings. Sold through museum shops, home furnishing stores, and craft galleries, her line of Photo Vellum lamps features over thirty images ranging from bucolic to architectural and industrial landscapes.

Alva by Starfish   pages 49, 91
4 Ella Mews
Cressy Road
London NW3 2NH
44 (0)20 7267 5705/Fax: 44 (0)20 7267 7086
Email: alva@isisdes.demon.co.uk
www.alva.uk.net
Alva is the lighting range manufactured by the British company Stafish Designs Ltd. Starfish was established in 1997 to develop a series of products which offer good design at affordable prices. Available to the trade.

Andromeda   pages 55, 101
Spot R.P. Via Beatrice D'Este
26- Milano T.
0039 02 58322585/Fax: 0039 02 58322587
rp@iol.it
This Venetian manufacturing company seeks to keep the Murano glass-making tradition alive while looking at the contemporary needs of today's consumer. Available to the trade/and through international retailers. US. Agent: Spazio Architettonico, South Miami, Florida: 305-373-2949.

Aqua Creations   pages 53, 65-66, 95
69 Mazeh St.
Tel-Aviv, Israel 65789
Email: info@aquagallery.com
www.aquagallery.com
U.S. representative: Stephanie Odegard Co., 200 Lexington Ave., Suite 1206, New York, NY 10016, 212-545-0069/Fax: 212-545-0298; limor@aquagallery.com.
The Aqua Creations line consists of handmade lamps and lighting sculptures designed by Ayala Serfaty, who has won international acclaim for her designs. She uses crushed Indian silk with organic metal forms. Available in select upscale stores and showrooms nationwide.

Archaic Smile, Inc.   pages 5-6, 43, 107
3157 Tchoupitoulas Street
New Orleans, LA 70115
Ph/Fax: 504-895-9028
Email: archaicsmile@archaicsmile.com
www.archaicsmile.com
Contact: Jeff Gladhart
Archaic Smile has been in business for over thirteen years, experiencing transformations from vintage store to nightclub and various other endeavours. Four years ago, Rachel Williams and Jeff Gladhart delved into housewares, creating lamps inspired by vintage designs. All shades are handprinted and bases are original designs. Available to the trade.

Benza, Inc.   page 95
413 West 14th St #301
New York, NY 10014
212-243-4047/Fax: 212-243-4689
E-mail: benzainc@aol.com
Italian slang for "gasoline," the name Benza was chosen by a New York City based group of designers to embody their desire to create high-octane design, and to drive people to say "wow!"

biproduct   page 98
97 Fifth Avenue 4A
New York, NY 10003-1011
212-255-3033/Fax: 212-243-2894
biproduct@earthlink.net
www.biproduct.com
Husband-and-wife design team, Stuart Basseches, an architect, and Judith Hudson, a graphic designer, use their lighting to reflect an interest in both scientific and architectural principles. Available to the trade/retail.

Bone Simple Design   pages 28, 47, 70, 93-94
17 Little West 12th Street #309
New York, NY 10014
212-627-0876
E-mail: chadjacobs@earthlink.net
Designer Chad Jacobs draws his inspiration from images and textures found in nature. He finds materials that inspire him — glass, steel, acrylic, and others — and then combines and manipulates them into simple but interesting shapes. Custom designs available. Available to the trade/retail.

Casanova/Bjorlin   page 8
171 Pier Ave. Suite 125
Santa Monica, CA 90405
310-664-7097/Fax: 310-664-7098
Casanova/bjorlin creates modern classics using a three rules of design: lighting must be effortless, simple, and luxurious. Available to the trade, and at select showrooms and retail stores.

Cherry Tree Design   pages 16, 19-20
34154 East Frontage Road
Bozeman, MT 59715
406-582-8800/Fax 406-582-8444
E-mail: ctdmt@aol.com
www.cherrytreedesign.com
Available to the trade.

Chista   pages 71-73
537 Greenwich St.
New York, NY 10013
212-924-0394/Fax: 212-633-9138
E-mail: Chista@interport.net
Sell to the trade, showroom open to the public by appointment only.

Christopher Poehlmann Studio, Inc. pages 8, 32, 36, 64
727 102nd Avenue North
Naples, FL 34108
941-597-4800/Fax: 941-592-7408
E-mail: chrispoehlmann@bigfoot.com
www.go2naples.com/poehlmann
Christopher Poehlmann has been designing and manufacturing furniture and lighting since 1986. His studio-produced work occupies a unique place somewhere between art and design. Poehlmann overseas every area of production and signs and dates each item produced at his studio. Available to the trade/retail.

Cotule pages 18, 28, 41, 91
100 Water Street, Suite 503
Brooklyn, NY 11201
Tel/Fax: 718-246-5206
www.cotule.com
French-born designer Stephane Pagani is founder and creative director of this lighting design firm that focuses on creating custom lighting fixtures and large-scale lighting installations. He uses his architectural background to focus on site-specific approaches to lighting Available to the trade/retail.

Daniel Schreiber pages 77-78
333 Dublin Ave.
Columbus, Ohio 43215
Phone/Fax: 614-228-1364
Available to the trade.

David Howell & Company page 41
405 Adams Street
Bedford Hills, NY 10507
530-666-4080/Fax: 530-666-2721
Email: info@davidhowell.com
www.davidhowell.com
Capturing light, playing with form, and creating a sensual object have been the goals of David Howell as he has experimented with marbles and metal to come up with a variety of unique lighting fixtures. Available to the trade.

David Long pages 9, 30, 104
10318 Jardine Avenue
Sunland, CA 91040
818-352-3727/ Fax: 818-951-2868
Email: LampArtz@aol.com
Building on a career as a Hollywood prop fabricator, David Long began to create zany lamps in the early 1990s. His products came out at a time when, Long said, the consumer was becoming "far more design conscious than that of a generation ago. No longer is having merely a source of illumination sufficient; nowadays, the source of the light must itself be sculptural, have some design congruity to the environment or, at the least, be non-obtrusive." Commissions and custom designs. Available to the trade/retail.

Decorative Crafts Inc. pages 13, 14
50 Chestnut Street
Greenwich, CT 06830
203-531-1500/Fax: 203-531-1590
E-mail: info@decorativecrafts.com
www.decorativecrafts.com
Established in 1928, Decorative Crafts Inc. produces classic designs in lighting fixtures. Available to the trade only.

Dez Ryan Studio pages 1, 15, 48, 54
475 Keap Street
Brooklyn, NY 11211
Ph/Fax: 718-486-5828
E-mail: dezryan@mindspring.com
www.dezryanstudio.com
A former sculptor, Dez Ryan works with glassblowers who craft the bodies of her lamps to spec, as well as with custom lampshade makers to create her exaggerated, exuberant forms using boldly patterned silks and exotic textiles. Available to the trade/retail.

Donovan Design pages 6, 43, 60, 78-80
127 Little Fresh Pond Road
Southampton, NY 11968
631-283-8175/Fax: 631-283-8175 +999
Art Donovan began his career in industrial design in 1977. Inspired by their honeymoon in Key West, he and his wife, Leslie Tarbell-Donovan, set out to establish a line of brightly colored, tropical deco table and accent lamps. Their collection includes over sixty original lighting designs, caviar bars, illuminated paintings, handmade clocks, illuminated cigar tables, custom chandeliers and screens. Each piece is handmade, signed and dated by Art Donovan.

Emily McLennan pages 56, 100
701 North Third Street
Minneapolis, MI 55401
612-339-7746/Fax: 612-333-3424
Designer Emily McLennan's Ladylite lamps utilize hand-turned wooden bases with just a few simple curves to suggest voluptuous female figures, topped by unfussy paper or corrugated fabric lamp shades. Available to the trade.

Estiluz, Inc. pages 81-84
235 Moonachie Road
Moonachie, NJ 07074
201-641-1997
Fax: 201-641-2092
www.estiluz.com
E-mail: estiluzinc@aol.com

Fantarte: Fancy Art Made in Italy pages 6, 9, 10, 16, 30-31, 63, 75, 80-81
Via Val Saviore
52 - 25132 Brescia, Italy
Tel/Fax 39-030314715
E-mail: unpul@tin.it
www.geocities.com/Yosemite/Trails/2304/fantarte.html
Custom designed works. Accept color requests from customers.

Fire & Water Lighting pages 48, 52, 58, 88, 95
241 Eldridge Street 3R
New York, NY 10002
212-475-3106/Fax: 212-677-7291
email: info@cyberg.com
www.cyberg.com
Architect David Bergman likes to use contrasts in his lighting designs, such as fluid and solid, organic and geometric, grace and strength, "fire and water." Environmentally conscious design — recycled materials, low VOC finishes, and energy efficient light sources — is also emphasized. Custom design and installation available. Available to the trade/retail.

MacKenzie-Childs, Ltd. page 14
Route 90
Aurora, NY 13026
212-947-3507/Fax: 212-947-4503
www.MacKenzie-Childs.com
Hand-made by artisans in a production studio on the eastern shore of Cayuga Lake, MacKenzie-Childs produces colorful, whimsical lighting. The company has a retail outlet in Manhattan (212-570-6050) and it sells via its website and regional merchants.

Manic Creative Art & Design page 90
3669 Nineteenth Street
San Francisco, CA 94110
415-640-1360
Email: bethweintraub@netscape.net
www.26keys.com/manic
Designer Beth Weintraub married her two biggest passions — furniture and fine art etchings — and then forged ties with Bay Area welders, glass blowers, and fine wood craftsman to execute her creations, now displayed in galleries and boutiques.Other etched metal products include counter tops and back splashes, home accessories, and fine art prints. Available to the trade/retail.

Mark Lee Lighting page 74
200 Bowery #8D
New York, NY 10012
212-925-6253/Fax: 212-219-9968
info@marklee.net
www.marklee.net
Mark Lee's dramatic style vividly transforms metal, fabric, and paper into lighting objects for commercial and residential interiors. Available to the trade.

Marre Moerel pages 37, 68, 92
182 Ilester Street #13
New York, NY 10013
Ph/Fax: 212-219-8985
Email: marremoerel@rcn.com
With a master's degree in furniture design, and an honorary degree in sculpture, from The Royal College of Art and Design in London. She taught furniture design at Parson's School of Art and Design and works and exhibits as both a fine artist and designer. In her lighting work, fine art and design mesh.

McLain Wiesand Custom Built Furniture pages 11, 28
1013 Cathedral St.
Baltimore, MD 21201
410-539-4440/Fax: 410-539-4448
e-mail: dwiesand@gateway.net
www.mclainwiesand.com
McLain Wisand designs and fabricates custom built furniture, lighting, and accessories with a strong neoclassical influence. One-of-a-kind or small quantities. Many original molds of decorative items and finials. They have a showroom at the address above, and are represented by the Wasington Design Center, 202-646-1540.

Michel Harvey Cèramique Inc. page 43
P.O. Box 445
Youville Station
Montreal Canada H2P 2V6
Ph/Fax: 514-845-7464
Designer Michel Harvey's hand-crafted porcelain containers double as flower vases when not wired for light. Available to the trade.

Nelson pages 94, 100-101
P.O. Box 17357
London SW9 OWB
England
Ph/Fax: 44 (0)208 5198694
E-mail: jfnelson1@aol.com
http://members.aol.com/nelsonpage
Inspired by the organic modernism of the 1950s, designer Julie Nelson launched her "Anthropoid" collection of lights in 1995. Her sculptural lights have since received widespread press coverage internationally. Available to the trade.

Ochre page 78
22 Howie Street
London SW11 4AS
England
44 (0)20 171 2238888/Fax: 44 (0)20 171 2238877
E-mail: enquiries@ochre.net
www.ochre.net
Ochre is a London-based design company striving to create objects of style and beauty which are both timeless and contemporary using high-quality natural materials, flawless craftsmanship, and good proportion. Their main collection consists of lamps,mirrors, stools, tables, screens, and panels. Available to the trade.

Olafur Thordarson/Dingaling Studio Inc. page 100
71 Broadway #13D
New York, NY 10006
212-979-2325/Fax: 212-863-9741
E-mail: olafurt@worldnet.att.net
www.dingaling.net
Designer Olafur Thordarson uses unconvention materials and methods to create his objects. Dingaling Studio is a multidisciplinary company dedicated to architecture, design, fashion, and art.

Pearce S. Lashmett page 47
44 Prospect Park West, #A9
Brooklyn, NY 11215
917-318-7157/Fax: 217-742-9503
E-mail: lashmett@aol.com
www.productny.com
A young designer from Illinois, Pearce Lashmett moved to New York City to pursue a degree in Product Design at Parsons School of Design in 1995 and graduated in 1999. He works as a product designer for a custom hardware manufacturer in New York. He enjoys exploring different or unexpected materials, and tries to fashion lighting that "creates an atmosphere for the space in which it lives." Available to the trade/retail.

Penta SRL page 37, 40, 56, 102
22060 Cabiate (Co)
Via Martin Luther King, 8
Italy
031-766100/Fax: 031-756102
E-mail: info@penta-lucearredo.it
www.penta-lucearredo.it

Prisco Studio page 89
36 E. 45th Street
Savannah, Georgia 31405
912-236-1450
art4m@msn.com
Richard Prisco creates one-of-a-kind and limited production lighting and furniture. His work explores structural solutions and their resulting aesthetic. He draws inspiration from bridges, architecture, and other civil and mechanical structures. Available to the trade/retail.

Reed Bros. page 70-71
Turner Station
Sebastopol, CA 95472
707-795-6261/ Fax: 707-823-5311
This small, northern California design studio manufactures made-to-order, hand-made and hard-carved wooden furniture and accessories for gardens, homes, hotels, restaurants, and resorts. Available to the trade.

Resolute pages 55, 96-98
1013 Stewart Street
Seattle, WA 98101
206-343-9308/Fax: 206-343-9322
E-mail: dpk@manifestocorp.com
Resolute, a registered trademark of Manifesto Corporation, has a state-of-the-art glass production studio to manufacture hand-blown glass, designing and producing innovative and functional lighting of quality.

Schonbek Worldwide Lighting pages 11-13, 60-61
61 Industrial Blvd.
Plattsburgh, NY 12901-1908
800-836-1892/Fax: 518-563-4228
email: sales@schonbek.com
www.schonbek.com
Founded in 1870 in Bohemia, Schonbek is the largest crystal chandelier manufacturer in North America today. Every Schonbek is an original design with its own pedigree. Styles include traditional, contemporary, retro, and eclectic. Custom work available/to the trade.

Sculture in Luce pages 21-22, 30, 62-63
Via Monteverdi, 1
21040 Venegono Inferiore VA Italy
Ph/Fax: 0039-2-55193838
Domenico Ciani and Daniele Votta, friends and artists in Milan, try to recreate their childhood memories of nature and fairy tales. All of their works are hand made and colored, and treated with a resin finish to make them completely washable. They will happily duplicate all items shown, though exact replicas may not be possible. Available to the trade/retail.

Sirmos pages 29, 40, 58, 102-103
30-00 47th Avenue
Long Island City, NY 11101
718-786-5920/Fax: 718-482-9402
e-mail: mail@sirmos.com
www.sirmos.com
Sources for the transformation of light are the primary focus of Sirmos, which designs and manufactures an innovative, sylish, and wide-ranging collection of interior lighting products, as well as the execution of custom products. They have a showroom in New York City, and representative showrooms in major cities around the country. To the trade.

Spaced Out, Ltd. page 42
46 Penton Street
London N1 9QA
Contact: Zach Pulman
44 (0)171 833 9236/Fax 44 (0)171-833-9237
E-mail: in@spacedout.demon.co.uk
www.spacedout.co.uk
Manufactured and distributed in the United States by Multi Media Electronics, Inc., 220 Verdi Street, Farmingdale, NY 11735; 516-847-7711/Fax: 516-847-7715.

Tiny Flame Studio page 36
550 Magnolia Avenue
Larkspur, CA 94939
Ph/Fax: 415-924-3401
Works by designer Grace Del Valle. To the trade.

Trout Studios pages 65, 67
5880 Blackwelder Street
Culver City, CA 90232
310-202-8896/Fax: 310-202-8896
www.troutstudios.com
Available to the trade.

W.A.C. Lighting pages 85-86
615 South Street
Garden City, NY 11530
800-526-2588/Fax: 800-526-2585
E-mail: sales@waclighting.com
www.waclighting.com
A leading manufacturer and designer of track and recessed lighting, undercabinet, and linear lighting, pendants, display lights, and rope lights. Available to the trade through regional dealers.

Wish Designs page 66
Road #5 Box 271
Sunset Valley
New Castle, PA 16105
724-458-4811/Fax: 724-458-9286
Email: wish at pathway.net
Deanna Wish uses natural hickory branches to create sconces, chandeliers, and table lamps. Her chandeliers span a petite 24 inches to hall-size six-foot diameter spans. All lighting is UL approved. Available to the trade/retail.

Worlds Away pages 14, 17-18
397 South Front Street
Memphis, TN 38103
901-529-0844/Fax: 901-527-3406
e-mail: bberry@worlds-away.com
www.worldsaway.com
Worlds Away is a seven-year-old company. All product is handpainted tin in Memphis, TN. The designs are exclusive and UL approved. 500 different lamps are available. Available to the trade.

Yayo! Designs, Inc. page 47
5-26 47th Avenue
Long Island City, NY 11101
718-482-8710/Fax: 718-482-8739
E-mail: yayo@jps.net
www. yayodesigns.com
Available to the trade.

Zumaluma, Inc. pages 44, 46
121 Gulf Road
Belchertown, MA 01007
Ph./Fax: 413-256-0509
Zumaluma, Inc. produces a line of paper lamps designed by celebrated artist Elsie Crawford. In keeping with Crawford's philosophy of simplicity and economy, each is made with a single sheet of paper, folded and/or bent to form a graceful paper sculpture. Crawfrod's work is in the permanent collections of the Los Angeles County Museum and the Oakland Museum of California. Available to the trade/retail.

LIGHTING
2000

TINA SKINNER

Schiffer Publishing Ltd

4880 Lower Valley Road, Atglen, PA 19310 USA

Copyright © 2000 by Schiffer Publishing
Library of Congress Catalog Card Number: 00-101870

Cover design by Bruce Waters
Book design by Blair Loughrey
Type set in Microgamma/Zurich

ISBN: 0-7643-1156-5
Printed in China

Published by Schiffer Publishing Ltd.
4880 Lower Valley Road
Atglen, PA 19310
Phone: (610) 593-1777; Fax: (610) 593-2002
E-mail: Schifferbk@aol.com
Please visit our web site catalog at WWW.SCHIFFERBOOKS.COM

This book may be purchased from the publisher.
Include $3.95 for shipping.
Please try your bookstore first.
We are interested in hearing from authors
with book ideas on related subjects.
You may write for a free catalog.

In Europe, Schiffer books are distributed by
Bushwood Books
6 Marksbury Ave.
Kew Gardens
Surrey TW9 4JF England
Phone: 44 (0) 208 392-8585; Fax: 44 (0) 208 392-9876
E-mail: Bushwd@aol.com
Free postage in the U.K., Europe; air mail at cost.

Title page photo courtesy of Dez Ryan Studio.